TWO *in* ONE
DESSERTS

Also by Hayley Parker:

Out of the Box Desserts

TWO *in* ONE DESSERTS

Cookie Pies, Cupcake Shakes,
and More Clever Concoctions

HAYLEY PARKER

The Countryman Press
A division of W. W. Norton & Company
Independent Publishers Since 1923
New York   London

I dedicate this book to my loyal, rockstar readers!
Without you, this wouldn't be possible.

For information about permission to reproduce selections from this book, write to
Permissions, The Countryman Press, 500 Fifth Avenue, New York, NY 10110

For information about special discounts for bulk purchases, please contact
W. W. Norton Special Sales at specialsales@wwnorton.com or 800-233-4830

The Countryman Press
www.countrymanpress.com

A division of W. W. Norton & Company, Inc.
500 Fifth Avenue, New York, NY 10110
www.wwnorton.com

978-1-68268-052-0

10 9 8 7 6 5 4 3 2 1

CONTENTS

Introduction

Have you ever been at a party or bakery and wanted multiple desserts at one time? But then you start to question whether it's socially acceptable to order tons of desserts and eat bites of each one? First, come to parties and bakeries with me, because I do order everything; and second, this book will be your best friend.

The idea for *Two in One Desserts* came to me in 2011 when I first started my food blog, *The Domestic Rebel*, and was dreaming of writing my very own cookbook. Because my blog was still a tiny blip on the map, I decided I'd create some of my recipes into mash-ups of sorts: combining two different desserts into one mega-dessert! My blog has a healthy mixture of classic dessert recipes and mash-up recipes, and my first cookbook, *Out of the Box Desserts*, focused on both, too. But I longed for a book that would allow me to exercise my creativity even further and create one-of-a-kind, two-in-one desserts exclusively!

That is precisely where *Two in One Desserts* delivers! Each recipe consists of two independent desserts that collide into one unique finished dish. I really wanted this book to be something that anyone—from novice home cooks to experienced chefs—could enjoy, from the food photography to the inventive recipes. Use this book as a guide to baking, but also as a guide to thinking outside the box and experimenting in the kitchen. Baking should be fun, and let's face it, desserts need to befriend one another a little better and stop being so straight and narrow. Why *can't* there be pie ice cream (or *pice cream*, as I obnoxiously call it)? Why *can't* I have a brownie-stuffed chocolate chip cookie? LET ME LIVE.

The question I get asked most often is, "So . . . what do you do with all of your desserts?" And the answer is . . . complicated and will have a long-winded answer. Bear with me.

You know that saying "Live to eat, or eat to live"? I'm in the former camp and always have been. Never have I ever been broken up and was so sad I couldn't eat, and never have I *ever* forgotten to eat. Food is my soul, my life's blood. I mean, when has a pint of ice cream *not* been there for you? EXACTLY MY POINT.

So, yes, I try everything I make. I may not *eat* everything I make, because they don't make pant sizes at the mall for size eleventy thousand. I should know, because I've checked. But whatever I don't scarf down at record speed, my dad or mom will take to work. Or I sometimes take it to the people who work at my bank in hopes that they'll *accidentally* add more money to my account. It hasn't happened yet, but I'm convinced if I continue to bribe them with treats, I'll *accidentally* be richer. It's called mind control, guys.

I bet you're wondering, *So how is this weirdo actually qualified to run a baking website?* And the answer is: It's called mind control, guys. No, but really, I'll tell you a little about myself.

I grew up cooking with my great-grandmother in her quaint kitchen in Paris, hand-kneading homemade croissant dough to the sound of chirping birds, buzzing bees, and the faint swoosh of lavender fields outside of her window.

Just kidding.

I grew up stealing spoonfuls of Cool Whip from my grandma's fridge when she was watching her stories. I stole Nutty Bars, Cosmic Brownies, and Circus Animal Cookies from the cupboard by actually army-crawling into the kitchen from the den and very quietly extracting the package from the box. I had Kraft Macaroni & Cheese for dinner probably three times a week. Oh, and my parents *never* cooked. The closest thing we had to croissants were refrigerated crescent rolls.

And the buzzing bees and swooshing lavender? My childhood home was nestled between a freeway on one side and train tracks on the other, so my family canceled out the noise of clanging trains with copious amounts of rock and roll blasted at full volume.

When I tell people that I grew up eating fast food for dinner so often that the lady at Carl's Jr. knew my order, they look at me as if they feel sorry for me. And to that I say: Don't! Because I got toys with every one of my meals and that means a lot when you're a kid. Also, because if I didn't get so sick of the drive-through window, I probably wouldn't have started my blog, which probably wouldn't have landed me here, with my book in your hands.

So, how did I go from drive-through diva to published cookbook author? I am entirely self-taught and have Food Network to thank for that. One day I turned on and watched an episode of a famous 30-minute-meal TV show and the rest was history! I went to the store, bought the ingredients, and taught myself how to mince, dice, sauté, and boil. I started cooking dinner for my family every night after I got home from high school. Instead of reading gossip magazines with my friends after school, I browsed recipe databases online for new recipes to try. Can you believe I even had *a* single friend? I did!

Cooking dinner every night segued into teaching myself how to bake. At first, the whole "baking is a science" thing scared me a little bit. But once I realized the magic you can make with a box of cake mix and your imagination running wild, I never looked back. And today, cake mix is still my inspiration and it's a prominent ingredient in this book because of its easiness, the fact that it's readily available, and because everyone needs a helping hand in the kitchen and cake mix is just a wonderful shortcut.

From Blueberry Muffin Cookies to Tiramisu Pie, Donut Upside-Down Cake to Blondie-Topped Brownies, you'll find 100 delectable mash-ups in this book, each specially created for all of you badass dessert rebels out there. No Parisian croissant-kneading necessary.

Happy baking!!
XO, Hayley

Kitchen Must-Haves

* Cake mix—any and every flavor! I always have white, yellow, and chocolate on hand. Cake mixes can vary in weight, between 15.25 and 18 ounces. Choose one within that range and you'll be good to go.

* Brownie mix—make sure it's a fudge brownie mix, which always yields the best results. See note about size of mixes, above.

* Instant (dry) pudding mix—I always have vanilla and chocolate ready to go! Just make sure they're instant, as cook & serve will not work. These come in a range from 3.4 to 3.9 ounces. They'll all work!

* Pie filling—an easy way to add fruit to a dessert! I like having cherry, apple, and berry available.

* Real butter—a must-have because it's the basis of so many recipes! And in most cases, there's no adequate substitution for it. All of my recipes call for unsalted butter, so you can control the amount of salt in the recipe. Salted butter may be used but then please omit the salt from the ingredients list.

* Vegetable or canola oil

* Large eggs

* Pure vanilla extract

* All-purpose flour

* Granulated sugar

* Brown sugar—dark or light! Dark will yield richer, more molasses-flavored results.

* Confectioners' sugar

* Baking soda

* Baking powder

* Cornstarch—my secret ingredient for fluffy cookies!

* Sprinkles, because you only live once!

* Heavy cream and milk

* Sweetened condensed milk

* Assorted baking chips—such as semisweet chocolate, vanilla, peanut butter, butterscotch, and dark chocolate chips

* Aluminum foil and parchment paper

* Cooking spray

* A 9-×-13-inch rectangular baking pan, an 8- or 9-inch square baking pan, two 9-inch round cake pans, a 9-inch springform pan, a Bundt pan, a 12-cavity muffin tin, and baking sheets

* Silicone liners—they make baking cookies easy!

* A cookie dough scoop (I like buying the tablespoon-size one)

* An electric mixer (stand mixer or hand-held)

These helpful tips and tricks will guide you through the prepping, baking, serving, and clean-up process swimmingly!

* To make cleanup a breeze, I line my pans with foil or parchment. To easily line a pan with foil, flip the pan over so it's upside down. Take a piece of foil that's larger than the pan and gently wrap the foil around the bottom and sides of the pan, fitting the foil into the shape of the pan. Gently remove the foil, flip the pan, and the foil will easily slide into the pan.

* To make cakes easier to remove from pans, line the springform or round cake pans with parchment rounds. Simply trace the pan's outline onto a piece of parchment paper and cut out the circle. Most stores sell parchment rounds that are even easier as they already come in a 9-inch circle!

* Muffin liners are a must-use for cupcakes and muffins. The best part is, you can customize the cupcake with a fun printed liner!

* I recommend using room-temperature butter for most of my recipes, unless otherwise specified. Leave it at room temperature for about 30 minutes to soften. Or in a pinch, microwave it, unwrapped, for 10 to 15 seconds.

* When measuring dry ingredients, such as flour and cake mix, spoon the dry ingredients into a measuring cup and level off the top with a butter knife to ensure the most accurate measurement.

* If you're melting chocolate, such as chocolate chips or chocolate bars, make sure none of your tools—the bowl, spoons, spatulas, etc.—have water droplets inside or on them. Even the tiniest droplet of water can cause chocolate to seize and harden, rendering it absolutely useless.

Successful Cookie
Tips and Tricks

* Some cookie recipes in this chapter require chilling. Chilling is mandatory, as it prevents the cookies from spreading while baking and it allows the flavors to develop. Trust me, I know you want cookies now—but the wait is worth it!

* I recommend lining the cookie sheets with parchment paper or silicone liners. This prevents cookies from sticking, of course, but also allows them to cook evenly. You can find silicone liners at most specialty food stores or craft stores.

* When baking cookies, rotate the pans halfway through the baking time to ensure even baking. If cooking two sheets at once, switch racks, too.

* Want the secret to perfectly round cookies? After I pull them out of the oven, I take a butter knife or offset spatula to gently push in the wonky edges that sometimes form during baking. I also like to sprinkle a few more chocolate chips or mix-ins on top of the cookies after baking.

* I recommend using a cookie dough scoop to portion out evenly sized balls of dough. I like using a 1-tablespoon size and a ¼-cup size, depending on how large I'd like the cookies.

Cookies

Who doesn't love cookies?! This chapter is one of my favorites because it's packed with amazing cookie recipes. From Birthday Cake to Almond Coconut, Brownie-Filled to Apple Pie, there's truly something for everyone!

Brownie-Filled Chocolate Chip Cookies

There are some things you have to choose in life. But there are others where you should put on your evil genius cap and combine your choices so you don't have to choose. That's sage advice from me, Miss Indecisive; you're welcome. That happens to be the case for these Brownie-Filled Chocolate Chip Cookies, which combine the classic cookie with a brownie center. Trust me, they're just as good as they sound! **12 COOKIES**

INGREDIENTS

12 tablespoons (1½ sticks) unsalted butter, at room temperature

1 cup brown sugar

½ cup granulated sugar

1 large egg

1 large egg yolk

1 tablespoon pure vanilla extract

1 teaspoon baking soda

2 teaspoons cornstarch

½ teaspoon salt

2 cups all-purpose flour

1½ cups semisweet chocolate chips

6 store-bought brownie bites

1. Cream together the butter and brown and granulated sugars in a large bowl, using an electric mixer, until creamy, about 2 minutes. Beat in the egg and egg yolk, followed by the vanilla. Beat in the baking soda, cornstarch, salt, and flour, beating well into a thick dough. Fold in the chocolate chips.

2. Cover and chill the dough in the fridge for at least 2 hours, up to overnight.

3. Preheat your oven to 350°F. Line two cookie sheets with silicone liners or parchment paper; set aside. Using a 2-tablespoon-size cookie scoop, scoop out some dough. Using your palms, gently flatten the dough a little bit. Place half of a brownie bite in the middle of the cookie dough and, using your hands, roll the dough around the brownie bite until the cookie dough is round again.

4. Drop the cookie dough balls on the prepared cookie sheets, spacing them about 2 inches apart. Bake for 10 to 12 minutes, rotating the pans halfway through the baking time to ensure even cooking. Remove from the oven and allow to cool completely on the baking sheets before serving.

Pecan Praline Cookies

I'm a California girl through and through, but I've longed to visit the South to get some of that good ol' southern food. One food that tops my must-have list is pralines, those irresistible southern cookies/candies. They melt in your mouth, are filled with pecans, and are a staple in southern food. Once I had the chance to try them in the Atlanta airport, I jumped on it and I've been hooked since. Since traditional pralines require candy thermometers and special powers to make, these cookies are the next best thing!

18–20 COOKIES

INGREDIENTS

1 box butter pecan cake mix

½ cup vegetable or canola oil

2 large eggs

8 tablespoons (1 stick) unsalted butter

1 cup brown sugar

¼ cup heavy cream

2 cups confectioners' sugar

1 cup chopped pecans

1. Preheat your oven to 350°F. Line two cookie sheets with silicone liners or parchment paper and set aside.

2. Mix together the cake mix, oil, and eggs in a large bowl until a thick, soft dough forms. Drop heaping, rounded tablespoonfuls of dough onto the prepared cookie sheets, spacing them about 2 inches apart. Bake for 8 to 10 minutes, rotating the pans halfway through the baking time to ensure even cooking. Remove from the oven and allow to cool completely.

3. Bring the butter and brown sugar to a boil in a medium saucepan, stirring constantly for exactly 2 minutes. Add the cream and bring the mixture back to a boil. Remove from the heat immediately and allow to cool slightly, about 15 minutes. Add the confectioners' sugar and pecans and whisk until a thick frosting forms.

4. Spread a heaping 1 to 2 tablespoons of frosting on each cookie. Let set for about 10 minutes before serving.

Crumb Apple Pie Cookies

This very well may be my favorite recipe in the book. Okay, one of my (many) favorites. I love them so much because apple pie happens to be my favorite flavor of pie, and because combining apple pie into cookies is kind of a stroke of brilliance, don't ya think? Crumb Apple Pie is my favorite because crumbs make the best addition to pies, in my humble opinion. If you don't like apple, try using a different flavor of pie filling, such as peach, cherry, or even blueberry. **36 COOKIES**

INGREDIENTS

Cooking spray

One package (2-count) refrigerated piecrusts, at room temperature

Two 21-ounce cans apple pie filling, chopped into smaller pieces (see Note)

2 cups all-purpose flour

¾ cup brown sugar

⅔ cup granulated sugar

¾ cup old-fashioned oats

1 teaspoon ground cinnamon

16 tablespoons (2 sticks) unsalted butter, melted

NOTE: You can substitute the canned pie filling with fresh apples, if preferred. Just peel and dice 4 cups of Granny Smith apples and sauté them with 3 tablespoons brown sugar, 2 teaspoons ground cinnamon, ¼ teaspoon ground nutmeg, and ¼ teaspoon ground ginger, in 2 tablespoons unsalted butter for 5 minutes.

1. Preheat your oven to 350°F. Liberally spray two 12-cavity muffin tins with cooking spray; set aside.

2. Roll out the piecrusts and, using a 2½-inch biscuit cutter, cut out circles from each piecrust. You should get about 12 circles per piecrust, equaling 24 total. Reroll the piecrust scraps and cut a remaining 12 circles, for a grand total of 36 circles.

3. Press a circle in the bottom and slightly up the sides of each prepared muffin cup. Top with a heaping tablespoonful or two of apple pie filling.

4. Mix together the flour, brown sugar, granulated sugar, and oats in a medium bowl, using a fork. Pour in the melted butter and toss together until moistened. Drop 2 to 3 tablespoonfuls of the mixture on top of each crust in the muffin cups, gently pressing it down with the back of the measuring spoon to compact it into the cup.

5. Bake for 18 to 22 minutes, until the tops are light golden brown and the centers are bubbly. Remove from the oven and allow to cool in the baking pans for 15 to 20 minutes, then use a butter knife to gently run around the edge of the muffin cavity to release them. Repeat with remaining 12 cookies, respraying the muffin tin with cooking spray, if necessary.

Brownie Cookies

My sister loves to "à la mode" nearly every dessert, and who can blame her? When has ice cream not improved a dessert? Exactly. Her favorite thing to "à la mode" would be cookies. Whether they're chocolate chip, peanut butter, or sugar, she tops nearly every cookie I bake with a scoop of ice cream for good measure. When I made these Brownie Cookies, she was superexcited to try the unique cross between chewy brownies and soft cookies. These cookies taste just like the chewy, slightly crisp edge of a brownie and yes, they taste amazing à la mode. **18–20 COOKIES**

INGREDIENTS

1 box fudge brownie mix

⅓ cup all-purpose flour

¼ cup vegetable or canola oil

2 large eggs, beaten

2 tablespoons milk or water

1 cup semisweet chocolate chips

1. Preheat your oven to 350°F. Line two cookie sheets with silicone liners or parchment paper; set aside.

2. Mix together the brownie mix, flour, oil, eggs, and milk in a large bowl, using a spatula or spoon, until a very thick dough forms. Make sure you incorporate all the flour or brownie mix at the bottom of the bowl. Fold in the chocolate chips.

3. Drop heaping tablespoonfuls of rounded dough balls about 2 inches apart on the prepared cookie sheets. Bake for 8 to 10 minutes, until the tops of the cookies appear mostly set. They may look a little underdone, but do not overbake them as they will continue to cook as they sit on the baking sheet. Remove from the oven and allow the cookies to cool completely, or serve them slightly warm with ice cream.

Carrot Cake Gooey Cookies

Now, it's no secret that carrot cake isn't my favorite. But when I was thinking of recipes for this book, I knew I had to include carrot cake in here since most people love it. What can I say? I'm a good team player. I obviously tasted every recipe in this book and I have to admit: I loved these cookies! They're spicy, sweet, and utterly gooey. If you love carrot cake, you'll flip for these! And if you don't like carrot cake? Give them a try and you'll change your tune! 20–24 COOKIES

INGREDIENTS

1 box carrot cake mix

One 8-ounce package cream cheese, at room temperature

16 tablespoons (2 sticks) butter, at room temperature

1 large egg

1 teaspoon ground cinnamon

1 cup confectioners' sugar

1. Preheat your oven to 350°F. Line two cookie sheets with silicone liners or parchment paper; set aside.

2. Beat together the cake mix, cream cheese, butter, egg, and cinnamon in a large bowl, using an electric mixer, until combined. Using a tablespoon-size cookie dough scoop, scoop tablespoonfuls of dough into your hand and coat completely in the confectioners' sugar. Place the coated cookie dough balls on the prepared cookie sheets, spacing them 2 inches apart.

3. Bake for 10 to 12 minutes, rotating the pans halfway through the baking time to ensure even cooking. Remove from the oven and allow to cool completely on the baking sheets before serving.

Molten Lava Cake Cookies

Everyone's heard of molten lava cake, but have you heard of Molten Lava Cake Cookies? Tender, chocolaty cookies filled with molten lava, a.k.a. Nutella. No one will suspect these seemingly "normal" looking chocolate cookies are filled with a molten center. I'm assuming this cookie recipe is exactly what they meant by the saying "don't judge a book by its cover." You'll need to freeze the Nutella ahead of time, so keep that in mind when planning. These are best served warm. **22–24 COOKIES**

INGREDIENTS

1½ cups (6 ounces) Nutella or similar chocolate hazelnut spread

16 tablespoons (2 sticks) butter, at room temperature

1 cup brown sugar

¾ cup plus ½ cup granulated sugar

2 large eggs

1 teaspoon pure vanilla extract

1 cup unsweetened cocoa powder

2 cups all-purpose flour

1 teaspoon baking powder

½ teaspoon salt

NOTE: These are best served warm, when they're the most gooey and moltenlike. As they cool, the molten filling will "absorb" into the cookie, but they're still delicious!

1. Drop heaping tablespoonfuls of the chocolate hazelnut spread onto a parchment-lined baking sheet. Freeze until firm, for at least 1 hour.

2. Preheat your oven to 350°F. Line two cookie sheets with silicone liners or parchment paper; set aside.

3. Cream together the butter, brown sugar, and ¾ cup of granulated sugar in a medium bowl, using an electric mixer, until fluffy, about 2 minutes. Beat in the eggs, one at a time, followed by the vanilla. Add the cocoa powder, flour, baking powder, and salt and beat until a thick dough has formed.

4. Using a 2-tablespoon-size cookie dough scoop, scoop out a ball of cookie dough and gently flatten it into a disk in the palm of your hand. Place a frozen ball of chocolate hazelnut spread in the center of the cookie dough disk. Using your fingers, gently pinch the cookie dough to envelope the chocolate hazelnut center, rolling it in your palms as you do, so it's completely enclosed. Dredge the cookie dough balls in the remaining ½ cup of granulated sugar.

5. Drop the cookie dough balls 2 inches apart on the prepared cookie sheets and bake for 10 to 12 minutes, rotating the pans halfway through the baking time to ensure even cooking. Remove from the oven and allow to cool for 5 to 10 minutes before serving.

Boston Cream Pie Cookie Cups

Truth be told, I've never actually had a Boston cream pie. And if you haven't either, I gather that it's actually a cake, not a pie, and it's served in Boston. Or so I think. Basically, it consists of two buttery yellow cake layers with a creamy vanilla custardlike filling in between them, covered in chocolate ganache frosting, which gives the cake a free pass for being mislabeled as a pie. These cookie cups combine the flavors of Boston cream pie into two-bite treats that are labeled appropriately, and can be served outside of Boston's city limits. **24 COOKIE CUPS**

INGREDIENTS

Cooking spray

One 24-count package refrigerated sugar cookie dough

1 box instant vanilla pudding mix

1 cup milk

4 ounces (½ [8-ounce] tub) frozen whipped topping, such as Cool Whip, thawed

1 cup chocolate frosting, warmed until pourable

1. Preheat your oven to 350°F. Liberally spray a 24-cavity miniature muffin pan with cooking spray. Place one sugar cookie dough cube into each muffin cavity and gently press down on each cookie dough cube with your fingers to flatten.

2. Bake for 10 to 12 minutes, until the cookies are golden brown and the centers appear just about set. Remove from the oven and allow to cool for about 15 minutes, then use the handle of a wooden spoon to gently make an indentation in each cookie cup's center. Allow to cool completely.

3. Whisk together the vanilla pudding mix and milk in a medium bowl for about 2 minutes, or until thickened. Fold in the whipped topping until fluffy and light.

4. Pipe the filling into each cookie cup, or use a tablespoon to drop a dollop of filling into each cookie cup. Drizzle with the pourable chocolate frosting.

Red Velvet Cake Cookies

Did you know that traditionally, red velvet cake was made with a cooked frosting and not a cream cheese frosting? Neither did I, until recently, when my world was opened up to cooked frosting land. It's glorious on this side of the frosting world, and I suggest you visit sometime. Cooked frosting is what tops these plush, fluffy cookies and makes them taste just like a good old-fashioned red velvet cake, just like Grandma used to make. Consider this your one-way ticket to Flavortown! **16–18 COOKIES**

INGREDIENTS

1 box red velvet cake mix

2 large eggs

½ cup vegetable or canola oil

¼ cup all-purpose flour

¾ cup milk

¾ cup sugar

12 tablespoons (1½ sticks) unsalted butter

1 tablespoon pure vanilla extract

Sprinkles for decoration (optional but recommended)

1. Preheat your oven to 350°F. Line two cookie sheets with silicone liners or parchment paper; set aside.

2. Stir together the cake mix, eggs, and oil in a large bowl until a thick dough has formed. Drop rounded tablespoonfuls of dough onto the prepared cookie sheets, about 2 inches apart. Bake for 8 to 10 minutes, rotating the pans halfway through the baking time to ensure even cooking. Remove from the oven and allow to cool completely.

3. Prepare the frosting: Whisk together the flour and milk in a medium saucepan over medium heat until thick, stirring constantly, about 5 minutes. Remove from the heat and allow to cool for 15 minutes.

4. Beat together the sugar, butter, and vanilla in a medium bowl until fluffy and creamy, about 1 minute. Beat in the flour mixture, a little at a time, until combined and smooth.

5. Spread a heaping 2 tablespoons of frosting on top of each cookie. Garnish with sprinkles, if using.

Blueberry Muffin Cookies

I know what you're thinking: blueberry muffins in a cookie?! But trust me; this recipe is one you absolutely should make! Once I discovered the concept of making cookies from a box of muffin mix, I was hooked and haven't looked back. These cookies are extra-special because they're topped with a buttery lemon glaze that totally drives home the blueberry flavor. They're soft, chewy, gooey, and just perfect. Start with these as your gateway into muffin cookies, then immediately try it with another muffin mix flavor! 20–22 COOKIES

INGREDIENTS

1 box blueberry muffin mix

¾ cup old-fashioned oats

⅓ cup plus 2 tablespoons vegetable or canola oil

¼ cup brown sugar

1 large egg, beaten

3 to 4 tablespoons milk

1½ cups confectioners' sugar

2 tablespoons unsalted butter, melted

½ teaspoon lemon zest

2 teaspoons fresh lemon juice

1. Preheat your oven to 375°F. Line two cookie sheets with silicone liners or parchment paper; set aside.

2. Stir together the muffin mix, oats, oil, brown sugar, beaten egg, and 2 tablespoons of the milk in a large bowl, using a spatula, until moistened and a thick dough has formed. Drop rounded tablespoonfuls of dough onto the prepared cookie sheets, about 2 inches apart.

3. Bake for 8 to 10 minutes, until the tops are light golden brown and the centers just appear set. They may look slightly underdone; this is okay, as you do not want to overbake them. Remove from the oven and allow to cool completely.

4. Whisk together the confectioners' sugar, melted butter, lemon zest and juice, and remaining 1 to 2 tablespoons of milk in a medium bowl until glossy and pourable. Drizzle the lemon glaze over each cookie. Allow the glaze to set, about 15 minutes, before serving.

Peach Pie Cookies

I know, I know—two pie cookie recipes? I love pie, so two is just the tip of the iceberg for me. These Peach Pie Cookies taste just like peach pie because they're made with piecrust and peach pie filling (duh). They remind me of a backyard barbecue in July—all-American, easy to make, cute to serve. Serve them up in a little basket lined with a red checkerboard napkin and a sprig of mint for some freshness. Or just eat them right off the cookie sheet; your choice. **10 COOKIES**

INGREDIENTS

One package (2-count) refrigerated piecrusts, at room temperature

1 cup peach pie filling, roughly chopped (see Note)

1 large egg, beaten

¼ cup cinnamon sugar (¼ cup sugar plus 2 teaspoons ground cinnamon, mixed)

NOTE: You can also use 1 cup peeled and diced fresh or thawed frozen peaches, tossed with 3 tablespoons brown sugar and 1 teaspoon ground cinnamon.

1. Preheat your oven to 350°F. Line two cookie sheets with silicone liners or parchment paper; set aside.

2. Roll out each piecrust sheet and, using a 3-inch round biscuit cutter, cut out circles from each sheet. You should have a total of 20 circles. Place 10 of the circles on the prepared cookie sheets, spacing them about 2 inches apart. Fill the center of each piecrust circle with a scant tablespoon of filling, trying to keep the filling as much in the center as possible.

3. Use a pastry brush or your finger to gently wet the perimeter of the piecrust circle with the beaten egg, then top with another piecrust circle. Use your fingers to press the edges together, then use a fork's tines to crimp the edges. Brush the tops with more egg and sprinkle with cinnamon sugar.

4. Bake for 20 to 25 minutes, until the cookies are golden brown and crisp. Remove from the oven and allow to cool completely before serving.

Lemon Bar Cookies

Lemon desserts are one of my favorites any time of year. They're refreshing in the summertime, but also cozy and wintry during the colder months. Lemon bars happen to be one of my favorites because they're a cinch to make and because they have the perfect balance of sweet and tart. These Lemon Bar Cookies taste just like lemon bars but are even easier to make, if you can believe it! And man, they may be my new favorite lemon dessert! 16–18 COOKIES

INGREDIENTS

One 17.5-ounce package sugar cookie mix

8 tablespoons (1 stick) unsalted butter, at room temperature

1 egg

Zest of 1 lemon

⅓ cup all-purpose flour

½ cup lemon curd (see Note)

Confectioners' sugar for dusting (optional)

NOTE: Don't stop at lemon curd! Use raspberry curd, orange marmalade, or lime curd in its place!

1. Preheat your oven to 350°F. Line two cookie sheets with silicone liners or parchment paper; set aside.

2. Mix together the sugar cookie mix, butter, egg, lemon zest, and flour in a large bowl, using a spatula, until blended. The mixture will be thick. Drop rounded tablespoonfuls of dough onto the prepared cookie sheets, about 2 inches apart. Make a small indentation in the center of each cookie, using your thumb or the bottom of a tablespoon. Fill with about a teaspoon of lemon curd.

3. Bake for 10 to 12 minutes, rotating the pans halfway through the baking time to ensure even cooking. Remove from the oven and allow to cool completely on the baking sheets. Dust with confectioners' sugar before serving, if desired.

S'mores Cookies

Gooey cookie lovers, please—make these bad boys! If you love the gooey, fluffy, chocolaty taste of s'mores, these cookies are a must-make. Chewy, ultrathick, and filled with pockets of chocolate and marshmallow, they're one of my go-to cookies for when I'm craving something sweet. Hopefully, you'll agree! 22–24 COOKIES

INGREDIENTS

12 tablespoons (1½ sticks) unsalted butter, at room temperature

1 cup brown sugar

½ cup granulated sugar

1 large egg

1 large egg yolk

1 tablespoon pure vanilla extract

1 teaspoon baking soda

2 teaspoons cornstarch

1 teaspoon salt

2 cups all-purpose flour

1 cup finely ground graham cracker crumbs

¾ cup semisweet chocolate chips

¾ cup marshmallow bits (see Note)

NOTE: Marshmallow bits are sold by the brand Jet-Puffed and are teeny-tiny dehydrated marshmallows. You can find them either in the baking aisle or near the hot chocolate.

1. Cream together the butter, brown sugar, and granulated sugar in a large bowl, using an electric mixer, until fluffy, about 2 minutes. Beat in the egg and egg yolk, beating well, followed by the vanilla. Beat in the baking soda, cornstarch, salt, flour, and graham cracker crumbs until a thick yet soft dough forms. Fold in the chocolate chips and marshmallow bits.

2. Cover and chill for at least 2 hours, up to overnight. Chilling is mandatory.

3. Preheat your oven to 350°F. Line two cookie sheets with silicone liners or parchment paper. Using a tablespoon-size cookie dough scoop, scoop out rounded balls of cookie dough and place on the prepared cookie sheets, about 2 inches apart. Bake for 8 to 10 minutes, until golden brown and the centers look just about set. They may look slightly underdone; this is okay as they will continue to cook as they cool. Do not overbake. Remove from the oven and allow to cool for at least 15 minutes before serving.

Almond Coconut Candy Cookies

I used to be in the coconut-loving minority in my family. But then some of my family members started to come around and like coconut, and now I have to share all my Almond Joy candy bars. (At least the stash they know about . . . *cue evil laugh*.) So, when I whipped up these cookies, you bet my family was clamoring for a taste. The worst part is, the first batch I made wasn't coconutty enough, so my poor fam had to sit through another round of recipe testing before I got it right. ("Poor fam," indeed). Now I'm happy to report that these cookies are the perfect amount of coconutty goodness . . . and taste just like Almond Joys! **24 COOKIES**

INGREDIENTS

One 17.5-ounce package sugar cookie mix

1 box instant coconut pudding mix

1 teaspoon coconut extract

8 tablespoons (1 stick) unsalted butter, at room temperature

1 large egg

2 to 3 tablespoons heavy cream or milk

½ cup chopped almonds

½ cup semisweet chocolate chips

½ cup shredded sweetened coconut

1. Preheat your oven to 350°F. Line two cookie sheets with silicone liners or parchment paper; set aside.

2. Mix together the sugar cookie mix, coconut pudding mix, coconut extract, butter, egg, and cream in a large bowl, using a spatula, until a soft yet thick dough forms.

3. Drop rounded tablespoonfuls of dough onto the prepared cookie sheets, about 2 inches apart. Bake for 8 to 10 minutes, rotating the pans halfway through the baking time to ensure even cooking. Remove from the oven and allow to cool completely before serving.

Birthday Cake Cookies

If you've been a member of the world in the past few years, you know that birthday cake-flavored treats are all the rage. From birthday cake macarons to birthday cake ice cream, everything has been birthday-ified . . . including chewing gum! These cookies are an homage to my love for all things cake batter. If you're craving that sweet cake flavor but don't feel like whipping up an entire cake (not an easy feat), these cookies are for you!

18–20 COOKIES

INGREDIENTS

1 box confetti cake mix

2 large eggs

8 tablespoons (1 stick) unsalted butter, at room temperature

½ teaspoon almond extract

1 teaspoon pure vanilla extract

¾ cup white chocolate chips

1. Preheat your oven to 350°F. Line two cookie sheets with silicone liners or parchment paper; set aside.

2. Mix together the cake mix, eggs, butter, and almond and vanilla extracts in a large bowl, using a spatula, until a soft yet thick dough forms. Fold in the white chocolate chips. Drop rounded tablespoonfuls of dough onto the prepared cookie sheets, about 2 inches apart.

3. Bake for 8 to 10 minutes, rotating the pans halfway through the baking time to ensure even cooking. Remove from the oven and allow to cool completely before serving.

Successful Cake and Cupcake
Tips and Tricks

* I highly recommend using the toothpick test when testing doneness for cakes and cupcakes. Insert a toothpick, skewer, or cake tester into the center of the cake or cupcake. If the toothpick comes out clean or with moist crumbs (not wet), it's done.

* Make sure you beat your cake batter ingredients very well so as to fully incorporate the ingredients. I like to scrape the bottom and sides of the mixing bowl to ensure I get all the dry ingredients blended in.

* When making frosting: If your frosting is too thick or almost pastelike, simply add a tablespoon of milk or heavy cream at a time, beating until the mixture is moistened, smooth, and spreadable.

* I recommend doubling the frosting recipe for most of these recipes if you intend on piping the frosting very high on the cupcakes, as shown in the photos.

2

Cakes and Cupcakes

Cakes and cupcakes are some of the most popular recipes on my website, and for good reason! A truly delicious cake or cupcake is hard to come by. Some cake is too dry or bland, or the frosting isn't good. Never fear! This chapter is filled with delectable recipes that are just right.

Cream-Filled Oatmeal Cupcakes

For a long time, I've had a serious love affair with Oatmeal Creme Pies. They are just too dang irresistible for me to bypass. You could even say they are my favorite snack cake of all the snack cakes. I'm not playing around, people! The combination of soft and chewy oatmeal cookies with that marshmallow-like frosting is perfection . . . and the flavor is the star of these cupcakes! 18–20 CUPCAKES

INGREDIENTS

FOR CUPCAKES

1 box spice cake mix

1 teaspoon ground cinnamon

½ cup vegetable or canola oil

3 large eggs

1 box instant vanilla pudding mix

FOR FROSTING & GARNISH

4 tablespoons (½ stick) unsalted butter, at room temperature

One 7-ounce jar marshmallow fluff

1 teaspoon pure vanilla extract

4 cups confectioners' sugar

3 to 4 tablespoons heavy cream

2 Oatmeal Creme Pies or similar snack cakes, chopped

1. Prepare the cupcakes: Preheat your oven to 350°F. Line two muffin tins with 18 to 20 paper liners; set aside.

2. Beat together the cake mix, cinnamon, oil, eggs, and vanilla pudding mix, and 1 cup of water in a large bowl, using an electric mixer, until combined and smooth, about 2 minutes. Portion the batter evenly among the prepared muffin cups, filling about three-quarters full.

3. Bake for 15 to 18 minutes, until a toothpick inserted near the center comes out clean or with moist crumbs. Remove from the oven and allow to cool completely.

4. Prepare the frosting: Cream together the butter, marshmallow fluff, and vanilla in a large bowl, using an electric mixer, until smooth, about 2 minutes. Gradually beat in the confectioners' sugar, 1 cup at a time, until the frosting is light and fluffy, beating in the heavy cream as needed to make the frosting spreadable.

5. Pipe or spread the frosting onto the cooled cupcakes and top with pieces of the chopped Oatmeal Creme Pies.

Bananas Foster Cupcakes

Will you believe me when I say that I've never had a proper bananas Foster before? I know—bad food blogger over here! But in California, bananas Foster isn't a very common dessert—it seems to be best found in New Orleans, where it originated (and to which I've never been!). One of these days, though, you can bet on me taking a trip down to NOLA to eat my way through the city and come home 10 sizes larger than when I arrived. My pants may not be ready for it, but I am! 22-24 CUPCAKES

INGREDIENTS

FOR CUPCAKES

1 box butter pecan cake mix

½ cup brown sugar

1 cup mashed banana (about 2 large bananas)

½ cup vegetable or canola oil

3 large eggs

FOR FROSTING & GARNISH

4 tablespoons (½ stick) unsalted butter, at room temperature

¼ cup caramel sauce

½ cup mashed banana

¼ teaspoon rum or rum extract

1 teaspoon pure vanilla extract

4 cups confectioners' sugar

Banana chips and additional caramel sauce for garnish

1. Prepare the cupcakes: Preheat your oven to 350°F. Line two muffin tins with 22 to 24 paper liners; set aside.

2. Beat together the cake mix, brown sugar, mashed banana, oil, eggs, and 1 cup of water in a large bowl, using an electric mixer, until combined and smooth, about 2 minutes. Portion the batter evenly among the prepared muffin cups, filling about three-quarters full.

3. Bake for 15 to 18 minutes, until a toothpick inserted near the center comes out clean or with moist crumbs. Remove from the oven and allow to cool completely.

4. Prepare the frosting: Cream together the butter, caramel sauce, and mashed banana in a large bowl, using an electric mixer, until smooth and creamy, about 1 minute. Beat in the rum and vanilla and 1 cup of the confectioners' sugar until blended. Gradually add the remaining 3 cups of confectioners' sugar until completely incorporated. The mixture will be light, fluffy, and spreadable.

5. Pipe or frost the frosting onto the cooled cupcakes and garnish with a drizzle of caramel sauce and a banana chip.

Peanut Butter and Jelly Cupcakes

For a hot minute, I wondered deeply about whether it was okay that I made two peanut butter and jelly recipes for my book. *Would adults like these recipes?* I pondered. *Would I be the laughing stock of the blogging community?* I thought. But then I realized, everyone has a soft spot for PB&J, unless you don't, in which case, move along to the next recipe! But those of us who celebrate this iconic flavor duo have to give these cupcakes a whirl!

18–20 CUPCAKES

INGREDIENTS

FOR CUPCAKES

1 box vanilla cake mix

1¼ cups milk

½ cup vegetable or canola oil

3 large eggs

1 box instant vanilla pudding mix

1 cup jam (I used grape, but strawberry or raspberry would work!)

FOR FROSTING & GARNISH

4 tablespoons (½ stick) unsalted butter, at room temperature

½ cup creamy peanut butter

1 teaspoon pure vanilla extract

3½ to 4 cups confectioners' sugar

¼ cup heavy cream

¾ cup jam

1. Prepare the cupcakes: Preheat your oven to 350°F. Line two muffin tins with 18 to 20 paper liners; set aside.

2. Beat together the cake mix, milk, oil, eggs, and vanilla pudding mix in a large bowl, using an electric mixer, until smooth and combined, about 2 minutes. Portion the batter evenly among the prepared muffin cups, filling about three-quarters full.

3. Bake for 15 to 18 minutes, until a toothpick inserted near the center comes out clean or with moist crumbs. Remove from the oven and allow to cool completely. Using a small paring knife or cupcake corer, core the centers of the cupcakes. Discard the cores. Fill the cupcakes evenly with the jam.

4. Prepare the frosting: Beat together the butter, peanut butter, and vanilla in a large bowl, using an electric mixer, until creamy and smooth, about 1 minute. Gradually beat in the confectioners' sugar until the frosting is smooth and fluffy, streaming in the cream until the frosting is of a spreadable consistency.

5. Pipe or spread the frosting onto the cooled cupcakes. Slightly warm the remaining jam and drizzle it over the frosting before serving.

Chocolate Chip Cookie Dough Brownie Bomb Cake

In 2013, I happened to invent the "brownie bomb"—a delectable confection made of egg-free cookie dough wrapped in a fudgy baked brownie and coated in chocolate. It went viral on the Internet for good reason—it's kind of bomb diggity, if you ask me! Over the years I've come up with different variations of the brownie bomb with fun new fillings to keep readers on their toes. But when I made this cake? The world went crazy yet again. Once you take a bite, you'll understand the phenomenon. 12–14 SLICES

INGREDIENTS

FOR BROWNIES

Cooking spray

2 boxes fudge brownie mixes, plus
  ingredients listed on back of boxes

FOR COOKIE DOUGH
FILLING & TOPPING

16 tablespoons (2 sticks) unsalted butter,
  at room temperature

¾ cup brown sugar

¼ cup granulated sugar

½ cup heavy cream

1 tablespoon pure vanilla extract

1 teaspoon salt

2 cups all-purpose flour (see Note)

2½ cups miniature chocolate chips

1 cup semisweet chocolate chips

NOTE: If you are worried about eating raw flour, use almond, quinoa, coconut, or oat flour.

1. Prepare the brownies: Preheat your oven to 350°F. Lightly spray two 9-inch round springform pans with cooking spray. Place a parchment round in the bottom of the pan. Spray the parchment and the pan yet again with cooking spray; set aside.

2. Prepare the brownie mixes according to the package directions, in separate bowls. Pour one bowl's worth of brownie batter into each pan. Bake for 30 to 35 minutes, until a toothpick inserted near the center comes out clean or with moist crumbs. Remove from the oven and allow to cool completely.

3. Prepare the cookie dough filling: Cream together the butter, brown sugar, and sugar in a large bowl until creamy, about 2 minutes. Beat in ¼ cup of the cream and the vanilla until combined. Finally, beat in the salt and flour until a soft dough forms. Fold in 1½ cups of the miniature chocolate chips.

4. Place a brownie "cake" layer on a plate or cake stand upside down. Top with the cookie dough and spread the dough out toward the edges of the cake. The cookie dough layer will be quite thick. Top with the remaining brownie "cake" layer.

5. Microwave the semisweet chocolate chips with the remaining ¼ cup of cream in microwave-safe bowl on HIGH, until melted and smooth, 30 to 45 seconds. Pour the ganache over the top of the brownie cake layer and smooth out to the edges. Sprinkle with the remaining cup of the miniature chocolate chips.

Chocolate Sandwich Cookie Cupcakes

There's a cake version of this recipe on my blog. When a reader reached out to me about whether it could be made into cupcakes, um, *hello*—that's genius! So, with a few tweaks, I made the cake in question into cupcakes and, man, was it a great suggestion! They're packed with lots of Oreo flavor and perfectly portion-size! 22–24 CUPCAKES

INGREDIENTS

FOR CUPCAKES

1 box chocolate cake mix

1¼ cups milk

⅔ cup vegetable or canola oil

3 large eggs

1 box instant Oreo-flavored pudding mix (see Note)

24 Oreo or similar cookies

FOR FROSTING & GARNISH

One 8-ounce package cream cheese, at room temperature

½ cup sugar

1 teaspoon pure vanilla extract

One 8-ounce tub frozen whipped topping, such as Cool Whip, thawed

2 cups crushed Oreo or similar cookies

Chocolate syrup

NOTE: If you can't find Oreo-flavored pudding mix, you can make your own by using instant vanilla pudding mix (one 3.4-ounce box) and ⅔ cup coarse crumbles of Oreo cookies.

1. Prepare the cupcakes: Preheat your oven to 350°F. Line two muffin tins with 22 to 24 paper liners; set aside.

2. Beat together the cake mix, milk, oil, eggs, and Oreo pudding mix in a large bowl, using an electric mixer, until combined and smooth, about 2 minutes. Portion the cookies evenly among the prepared muffin cups, and then portion the batter evenly atop the cookies, filling each cup about three-quarters full and covering the cookie in the bottom completely.

3. Bake for 15 to 18 minutes, until a toothpick inserted near the center comes out clean or with moist crumbs. Remove from the oven and allow to cool completely.

4. Prepare the frosting: Cream together the cream cheese, sugar, and vanilla in a large bowl until combined, about 1 minute. Fold in the whipped topping until thoroughly combined, and then fold in 1 cup of the crushed cookies. Cover and refrigerate for 1 hour.

5. Using a cookie dough scoop, scoop generous 1 to 2 tablespoonfuls of the frosting on top of each cupcake, ice-cream style. Make an indentation in the top of the frosting and drizzle on some chocolate syrup, then top with the remaining crushed cookies.

Chocolate Hazelnut Candy Cupcakes

These cupcakes remind me of something you'd find in an Upper East Side, NYC bakery. They are kind of outrageous, being drizzled with Nutella and topped with a whole chocolate-hazelnut truffle candy—but in an elegant way. (Kind of like NYC itself!) Moist chocolate cake topped with a Nutella buttercream frosting and a truffle candy. There are few things better than this cupcake! **18–20 CUPCAKES**

INGREDIENTS

FOR CUPCAKES

1 box devil's food cake mix

½ cup vegetable or canola oil

1¼ cups milk

3 large eggs

1 box instant chocolate pudding mix

2 teaspoons hazelnut extract, optional

FOR FROSTING, GARNISH, & TOPPING

4 tablespoons (½ stick) unsalted butter, at room temperature

½ cup plus ⅔ cup Nutella or similar chocolate hazelnut spread

1 teaspoon pure vanilla extract

3½ to 4 cups confectioners' sugar

¼ cup heavy cream

20 Ferrero Rocher or similar hazelnut truffle candies

1. Prepare the cupcakes: Preheat your oven to 350°F. Line two muffin tins with 18 to 20 paper liners; set aside.

2. Beat together the cake mix, oil, milk, eggs, chocolate pudding mix, and hazelnut extract, if using, in a large bowl, using an electric mixer, until combined and smooth, about 2 minutes. Portion the batter evenly among the prepared muffin cups, filling about three-quarters full.

3. Bake for 15 to 18 minutes, until a toothpick inserted near the center comes out clean or with moist crumbs. Remove from the oven and allow to cool completely.

4. Prepare the frosting: Cream together the butter, ½ cup of Nutella, and vanilla in a large bowl until creamy, about 2 minutes. Gradually add the confectioners' sugar, 1 cup at a time, alternating with the cream, until the mixture is light and fluffy.

5. Pipe or spread the frosting onto the cooled cupcakes. Drizzle with the remaining ⅔ cup of Nutella and top each with a Ferrero Rocher candy.

Key Lime Pie Cake with Graham Cracker Whipped Cream

The first time I went to Miami, I was on the hunt for two things: authentic mojitos and Key lime pie. I am happy to report that I successfully found both of those items and consumed both of those items religiously in my three-day stay. Prior to my trip, I hadn't really given Key lime pie a chance, and for that I'd like to publicly apologize. Key lime pie, I'm sorry I doubted your deliciousness, but I'm glad we could make amends. Now I love the stuff, and I especially love that bright, tart flavor in this cake! And the whipped cream? Let's just say a trough-full still wouldn't be enough. 12–14 SLICES

INGREDIENTS

FOR CAKE

Cooking spray

1 box white cake mix

3 large eggs

½ cup vegetable or canola oil

¾ cup milk

Zest of 3 limes (about 3 tablespoons)

½ cup fresh or bottled Key lime juice

One 6-ounce container lime yogurt

FOR WHIPPED CREAM

¾ cup heavy cream

¼ cup sugar

¼ cup graham cracker crumbs

1. Prepare the cake: Preheat your oven to 350°F. Liberally spray a 10-cup Bundt pan with cooking spray and set aside.

2. Beat together the cake mix, eggs, oil, milk, Key lime zest and juice, and lime yogurt in a large bowl, using an electric mixer, until combined and smooth, about 2 minutes. Pour the cake batter into the prepared Bundt pan and smooth out the top.

3. Bake for 45 to 55 minutes, until a toothpick inserted near the center comes out clean or with moist crumbs. Remove from the oven and allow to cool for 20 to 25 minutes in the pan, then carefully invert the cake onto a wire rack to cool completely.

4. Whip the cream and sugar together in a large bowl, using an electric mixer on medium-high speed, until stiff peaks form, 5 to 7 minutes. Fold in the graham cracker crumbs.

5. Serve the cake sliced with a dollop of whipped cream on the side.

Donut Upside-Down Cake

This is one of those recipes that health nuts will be horrified over . . . but you only live once, right? I'm sure you've heard of pineapple upside-down cake? This is the pineapple cake's crazy, estranged cousin who shows up to the parties unexpectedly. You think you know what you're going to get until the pan is inverted and *bam!*—there are donuts on the bottom instead of pineapple rings. Not for the faint of heart, this cake may be my favorite cake in this chapter! Why choose between donuts and cake when this recipe allows you to have both?! 12–14 SLICES

INGREDIENTS

FOR SAUCE

Cooking spray

8 tablespoons (1 stick) unsalted butter

¾ cup dark brown sugar

3 tablespoons heavy cream

1 cup chopped pecans

4 glazed yeast donuts, plus 5 to 6 glazed yeast donut holes

FOR CAKE

8 tablespoons (1 stick) unsalted butter

1 cup dark brown sugar

1 large egg

1½ cups all-purpose flour

2 teaspoons baking powder

½ cup milk

1 teaspoon pure vanilla extract

1. Prepare the sauce: Preheat your oven to 350°F. Spray a 9- or 10-inch round cast-iron skillet with cooking spray. Add all the sauce ingredients, minus the donuts, and cook over medium-low heat until melted and combined.

2. Place the donuts and donut holes into the pan, fitting them as tightly as possible and filling the gaps between the donuts with donut holes. Set aside to cool off, about 10 minutes.

3. Prepare the cake: Whisk together the milk and vanilla in a small bowl. Cream together the butter and dark brown sugar in a separate large bowl until fluffy, about 2 minutes. Beat the egg and baking powder into the butter mixture until combined. Alternate adding the flour and the milk mixture to the butter mixture until a soft cake batter forms. Pour the cake batter evenly over the donuts in the pan and smooth out the surface.

4. Bake for 35 to 45 minutes, until the cake is light golden brown and a toothpick inserted near the center comes out clean or with moist crumbs. Remove from the oven and allow to cool for 10 minutes in the pan, then very carefully (as the pan will still be very hot) invert the skillet onto a platter or plate. Let the skillet sit upside down on the platter for about 1 minute before gently removing it, revealing the cake on the platter. Serve while warm or at room temperature.

Pecan Praline Bundt Cake

Okay, so pecan pralines are one of my favorite treats, but I *never* have them. Why, you ask, would you deprive yourself of such a heavenly treat? The answer is: because California isn't up to the times with the latest in southern confections, unfortunately. California is all rah-rah quinoa desserts, and I'm over here, like, where can I find a decent praline? #firstworldproblems. But once I tried this cake—with its glorious praline icing—I satisfied that praline craving quickly. Just try not to inhale the icing with a spoon! 12–14 SLICES

INGREDIENTS

FOR CAKE

Cooking spray

1 box butter pecan cake mix

3 large eggs

½ cup vegetable or canola oil

1 box instant vanilla pudding mix

FOR FROSTING

8 tablespoons (1 stick) unsalted butter

1 cup brown sugar

½ cup heavy cream

2 cups confectioners' sugar

1 cup chopped pecans

1. Prepare the cake: Preheat your oven to 350°F. Liberally spray a 10-cup Bundt pan with cooking spray and set aside.

2. Beat together the cake mix, eggs, oil, vanilla pudding mix, and 1 cup of water in a large bowl, using an electric mixer, until combined and smooth, about 2 minutes. Pour into the prepared pan and smooth out the top.

3. Bake for 45 to 50 minutes, until a toothpick inserted near the center comes out clean or with moist crumbs. Remove from the oven and allow to cool in the pan for 20 to 25 minutes, then carefully invert the pan onto a wire rack to release the cake to cool the cake completely.

4. Prepare the frosting: Bring the butter and brown sugar to a boil together in a medium saucepot, stirring and boiling for 2 minutes. Add the cream and bring back to a boil, then immediately remove from the heat and allow to cool for about 15 minutes.

5. Whisk in the confectioners' sugar until a thick frosting forms; however, the frosting will remain pourable. Fold in the chopped pecans and pour the frosting over the cake.

Peanut Butter Crunch Cupcakes

Butterfingers remind me of the days when my Grammie Pat would take my siblings and me to the movies during hot summer months. Beforehand, we'd always go to the dollar store or a gas station to pick out a handful of candies that Grammie would sneak into the theater. And back in the '90s, Butterfinger made bite-size "bits" and I gobbled those up first. Since then, my love for Butterfinger candies knows no bounds, and it was the inspiration for these candylicious cupcakes! 20–22 CUPCAKES

INGREDIENTS

FOR CUPCAKES

1 box chocolate cake mix

1¼ cups milk

⅔ cup vegetable or canola oil

3 large eggs

1 box instant chocolate pudding mix

FOR FROSTING & TOPPING

8 tablespoons (1 stick) unsalted butter, at room temperature

½ cup creamy peanut butter

1 teaspoon pure vanilla extract

¼ cup heavy cream

3½ to 4 cups confectioners' sugar

1 cup crushed Butterfinger or similar candies

1. Prepare the cupcakes: Preheat your oven to 350°F. Line two muffin tins with 20 to 22 paper liners; set aside.

2. Beat together the cake mix, milk, oil, eggs, and chocolate pudding mix in a large bowl, using an electric mixer, until combined and smooth, about 2 minutes. Portion the batter evenly among the prepared muffin cups, filling about three-quarters full.

3. Bake for 15 to 18 minutes, until a toothpick inserted near the center comes out clean or with moist crumbs. Remove from the oven and allow to cool completely.

4. Prepare the frosting: Cream together the butter, peanut butter, and vanilla in a large bowl, using an electric mixer, until creamy, about 2 minutes. Gradually add the confectioners' sugar, adding 1 cup at a time, alternating with the cream, until the frosting is light and fluffy.

5. Pipe or spread the frosting onto the cooled cupcakes. Garnish with the chopped Butterfinger candies.

Whoopie Pie Cake

It was later in life when I tried the famed whoopie pie. If you're like I was and are scratching your head at the name, a whoopie pie is a soft, almost cakelike cookie sandwich filled with buttercream frosting. Simple but satisfying, those irresistible little pies were the inspiration for this gigantic Whoopie Pie Cake! 12–14 SLICES

INGREDIENTS

FOR CAKE

Cooking spray

1 box chocolate fudge cake mix

4 large eggs

½ cup vegetable or canola oil

1 cup buttermilk

1 cup full-fat sour cream

FOR FILLING & TOPPING

4 tablespoons (½ stick) unsalted butter, at room temperature

One 7-ounce jar marshmallow fluff

1 teaspoon pure vanilla extract

½ teaspoon salt

2 cups confectioners' sugar

½ cup heavy cream

¾ cup semisweet chocolate chips

1. Prepare the cake: Preheat your oven to 350°F. Liberally spray a 10-cup Bundt pan with cooking spray; set aside.

2. Beat together the cake mix, eggs, oil, buttermilk, and sour cream in a large bowl, using an electric mixer, until combined and smooth, about 2 minutes. Pour the batter evenly into the prepared pan and smooth out the surface.

3. Bake for 40 to 50 minutes, until a toothpick inserted near the center comes out clean or with moist crumbs. Remove from the oven and allow to cool in the pan for 20 to 25 minutes, then carefully invert the pan onto a wire rack to release the cake. Allow the cake to cool completely, then use a serrated knife to slice the cake in half horizontally.

4. Prepare the filling: Cream together the butter, marshmallow fluff, vanilla, and salt in a large bowl, using an electric mixer, for about 2 minutes or until fluffy. Gradually add the confectioners' sugar, 1 cup at a time, followed by ¼ cup of the cream. The mixture will be really light and fluffy.

5. Place one cake half onto a platter or cake stand and top with the marshmallow filling, smoothing it out just about ½ inch before the edge of the cake. Top with the remaining cake half, dome side up.

6. Microwave the chocolate chips and the remaining ¼ cup of cream together in a small microwave-safe bowl on HIGH, until melted and smooth, 20 to 30 seconds. Pour the ganache over the top of the cake, allowing it to drip down the sides.

Cake Batter Molten Lava Cakes

Everyone's had a chocolate molten lava cake at least once, right? But did you know you can also make white chocolate, lemon, or even chocolate peanut butter molten lava cakes? I know, it's a game-changer! You can even make your molten lava cake taste just like cake batter—the gooey, sprinkle-filled stuff we all lick off the beaters. These pint-size cakes are not just adorable, they're a sprinkle-packed, ooey-gooey wonder!

4–6 CAKES (DEPENDING ON SIZE OF RAMEKINS)

INGREDIENTS

Cooking spray

4 ounces white chocolate, chopped

8 tablespoons (1 stick) unsalted butter, at room temperature

1 cup confectioners' sugar

2 large eggs

2 large egg yolks

6 tablespoons all-purpose flour

1 teaspoon pure vanilla extract

½ teaspoon almond extract

¼ teaspoon salt

1 cup rainbow sprinkles

Ice cream, whipped cream, or additional rainbow sprinkles for garnish

1. Preheat your oven to 425°F. Liberally spray four to six ramekins with cooking spray. How many cakes you get out of the recipe depends on the size of your ramekins. A standard ramekin (where you'll get six cakes) is about 3 inches in diameter. Place the ramekins on a rimmed baking sheet to make it easier to transfer to and from the oven; set aside.

2. Microwave the chopped white chocolate and the butter together in a microwave-safe medium bowl on HIGH for 20 seconds. Stir, then melt for another 10 to 15 seconds, until completely smooth. Whisk in the confectioners' sugar until blended. Whisk in the eggs, egg yolks, flour, vanilla and almond extracts, and salt until a cohesive batter forms. Fold in the sprinkles.

3. Fill each ramekin equally with batter, filling one-half to two-thirds full. Bake for 12 to 15 minutes, checking at the 12-minute mark. The cake should look mostly set along the edges, but soft in the middle. If it's sloshing around in the pan, it still needs more time, but if it jiggles slightly, that's okay.

4. Remove from the oven and allow each cake to cool in its ramekin for at least 3 to 5 minutes, then carefully invert the ramekin (it will be hot) onto a plate. If the cake doesn't come out, gently run a knife around the edge of the cake to release. Top with ice cream, whipped cream, or additional rainbow sprinkles.

Cannoli Cupcakes

When I was brainstorming ideas for this book, I first wrote down a list of desserts that I wanted to remix. Things like: banana split, pecan pie, tiramisu, and of course, cannoli. Cannoli are an underrated dessert, in my humble opinion, and they deserve more recognition! Maybe it's because people are put off by the idea of making cannoli dough and frying it, or maybe it's because there aren't many tubular desserts. Either way, there's no frying and minimal tubes in this cupcake recipe, but all that classic cannoli flavor is still present! 20–22 CUPCAKES

INGREDIENTS

FOR CUPCAKES

1 box white cake mix

1¼ cups milk

½ cup vegetable or canola oil

3 large eggs

1 box instant French vanilla pudding mix

FOR FROSTING & TOPPING

5 tablespoons unsalted butter, at room temperature

6 ounces cream cheese, at room temperature

1 teaspoon pure vanilla extract

4 cups confectioners' sugar

¼ cup to ⅓ cup heavy cream

1½ cups miniature chocolate chips

8 pirouette cookies, cut into thirds (see Note)

NOTE: Pirouette cookies are long, tubular cookies with a flaky outer layer and often a fudge-filled interior. If you cannot find these cookies, garnish the cupcakes with a waffle cookie instead.

1. Prepare the cupcakes: Preheat your oven to 350°F. Line two muffin tins with 20 to 22 paper liners; set aside.

2. Beat together the cake mix, milk, oil, eggs, and French vanilla pudding mix in a large bowl, using an electric mixer, until combined and smooth, about 2 minutes. Portion the batter evenly among the prepared muffin cups, filling about three-quarters full.

3. Bake for 15 to 18 minutes, until a toothpick inserted near the center comes out clean or with moist crumbs. Remove from the oven and allow to cool completely.

4. Prepare the frosting: Cream together the butter, cream cheese, and vanilla in a large bowl, using an electric mixer, until creamy and smooth, about 1 minute. Gradually add the confectioners' sugar, 1 cup at a time, alternating with the cream, until the frosting is light and fluffy. You may not use all of the cream.

5. Pipe or spread frosting onto the cooled cupcakes and top with a sprinkling of miniature chocolate chips and one-third of a pirouette cookie.

Banana Split Cupcakes

Ice cream is one of my favorite go-to treats. Preferably soft-serve ice cream. I know that some ice cream purists are gasping in mock horror, but I really enjoy it when it's softer and creamy and luscious. Plus, it's easier to create over-the-top sundaes with soft-serve since it all kind of melts together in one gorgeous puddle of deliciousness. One of my favorite soft-serve flavors is banana, and I just have to top it with strawberry sauce, sprinkles, and a cherry so I have my very own banana split. I tell myself it's healthy because it's banana flavored . . . and don't you dare tell me otherwise! 24 CUPCAKES

INGREDIENTS

FOR CUPCAKES

1 box yellow cake mix

3 large eggs

½ cup vegetable or canola oil

1 cup milk

1 box instant banana pudding mix

1 cup mashed bananas (about 2 medium to large bananas)

FOR FROSTING & TOPPING

12 tablespoons (1½ sticks) unsalted butter, at room temperature

1 teaspoon pure vanilla extract

¼ cup seedless strawberry jam

4 cups confectioners' sugar

¼ cup plus ⅓ cup heavy cream

1 cup milk chocolate chips

Sprinkles, maraschino cherries, and nuts for topping

1. Prepare the cupcakes: Preheat your oven to 350°F. Line two muffin tins with 24 paper liners; set aside.

2. Beat the cake mix, eggs, oil, milk, banana pudding mix, and mashed bananas in a large bowl, using an electric mixer, until combined and smooth, about 2 minutes. Portion the batter evenly among the prepared muffin cups, filling about three-quarters full.

3. Bake for 15 to 18 minutes, until a toothpick inserted near the center comes out clean or with moist crumbs. Remove from the oven and allow to cool completely.

4. Prepare the frosting: Cream together the butter, vanilla, and strawberry jam in a large bowl, using an electric mixer, until creamy and combined, about 1 minute. Gradually add the confectioners' sugar, 1 cup at a time, alternating with the ¼ cup of cream until frosting is light and fluffy.

5. Pipe or spread the frosting onto the cooled cupcakes. Microwave the chocolate chips and remaining ⅓ cup of cream in a small, microwavable bowl on HIGH for 20 to 30 seconds, until smooth and melted. Drizzle the ganache over the top of each frosted cupcake and top with sprinkles and a maraschino cherry.

Carrot Cake Cheesecake Cake

INGREDIENTS

FOR CAKE

Cooking spray

2¼ cups all-purpose flour

1½ teaspoons baking powder

1 teaspoon baking soda

½ teaspoon salt

2 teaspoons ground cinnamon

½ teaspoon ground ginger

2 cups shredded carrot

1 cup brown sugar

½ cup granulated sugar

¾ cup full-fat sour cream

4 large eggs

1 cup vegetable or canola oil

1 teaspoon pure vanilla extract

FOR FILLING

One 8-ounce package cream cheese,
 at room temperature

⅔ cup granulated sugar

1 teaspoon pure vanilla extract

1 large egg

FOR GLAZE & TOPPING

4 ounces cream cheese, at room temperature

2 tablespoons fresh orange juice

½ teaspoon pure vanilla extract

2 cups confectioners' sugar

1 cup chopped pecans for garnish
 (optional)

1. Prepare the cake: Preheat your oven to 350°F. Liberally spray a 10-cup Bundt pan with cooking spray; set aside.

2. Whisk together the flour, baking powder, baking soda, salt, cinnamon, and ginger in a medium bowl. Set aside. Combine the shredded carrot, brown sugar, white sugar, and sour cream, in a large bowl, beating with an electric mixer until just combined. Beat in the eggs, one at a time, followed by the oil and vanilla, until mixture is combined. With the mixer running on low speed, add the flour mixture slowly until a soft batter has formed.

3. Prepare the filling: Beat together the cream cheese, sugar, vanilla, and egg, an a medium bowl, using an electric mixer, until combined and smooth.

4. Pour half of the cake batter into the prepared pan. Spoon the cheesecake filling around the middle of the cake batter in the pan, trying to keep the cheesecake away from the very middle or the sides, almost like a tunnel of cheesecake. Top gently with the remaining carrot cake batter.

5. Bake for 50 to 60 minutes, until a toothpick inserted near the center comes out clean or with moist crumbs. Remove from the oven and allow the cake to cool in the pan for about 30 minutes, then carefully invert the pan onto a wire rack to cool the cake completely.

6. Prepare the glaze: Stir together the cream cheese, orange juice, vanilla, and confectioners' sugar in a medium bowl until thick and combined.

7. Once the cake has cooled, top it with the glaze. I like to put the glaze in a piping bag, snip off the corner, and pipe it on in thick stripes around the cake. Top with chopped pecans if you'd like. Serve immediately or store leftovers in the fridge.

Whenever I go to that famous cheesecake restaurant, I am always super overwhelmed by the varieties of cheesecake alone. The fact that they make all these cheesecake flavors is a testament that the cheesecake chefs and I are cut from the same cloth. Always striving to make some new outrageous dessert mash-up, always wanting to outdo ourselves with our flavors. This cake is inspired by that restaurant's Carrot Cake Cheesecake, which has ribbons of carrot cake swirled throughout. This cake is moist, flavorful, and fluffy and has ribbons of cheesecake swirled throughout. Your move, cheesecake chefs! **12–14 SLICES**

Cinnamon Roll Sheet Cake

Cinnamon is easily one of my favorite flavors, and cinnamon rolls are easily one of my favorite treats. Whenever I'm in their presence, I am weak in the knees. They are just too tempting! This Cinnamon Roll Sheet Cake may take the . . . well, cake, over regular, predictable cinnamon rolls though. Swirled with a healthy helping of a brown sugar and cinnamon mixture, and topped with a smooth cinnamon roll icing, it's far easier to make than its rolled-up counterparts . . . but just as easy to eat! **16 SLICES**

INGREDIENTS

FOR CAKE

Cooking spray

1 box white cake mix

1/3 cup vegetable or canola oil

4 large eggs

1 cup full-fat sour cream

1 teaspoon pure vanilla extract

3 tablespoons brown sugar

2 teaspoons ground cinnamon

2 tablespoons all-purpose flour

FOR ICING

2 cups confectioners' sugar

1/4 cup milk

2 teaspoons pure vanilla extract

1. Prepare the cake: Preheat your oven to 350°F. Liberally spray a 9-×-13-inch rectangular baking pan with cooking spray; set aside.

2. Beat together the cake mix, water, oil, eggs, sour cream, vanilla, and 1/4 cup of water in a large bowl, using an electric mixer, until combined and smooth, about 2 minutes. Pour the batter into the prepared pan. Meanwhile, in a small bowl, whisk together the brown sugar, cinnamon, and flour until combined. Pour the brown sugar mixture evenly over the cake batter. Use a butter knife to swirl the brown sugar mixture into the cake batter.

3. Bake for 40 to 45 minutes, until a toothpick inserted near the center comes out clean or with moist crumbs. Remove from the oven and allow to cool for 20 to 25 minutes.

4. Prepare the icing: Whisk together the icing ingredients until smooth. Pour over the cake and let set about 15 minutes before cutting into slices.

Tiramisu Cupcakes

I do not remember the first time I tried tiramisu, but the second that flavor explosion hit my mouth, all bets were off. It was my new go-to dessert to order. I have a serious thing for fluffy whipped cream, chocolate, and coffee flavors together. And let me tell you—these cupcakes are out of this world and bring all those classic tiramisu flavors together into one fabulous cupcake. 18–20 CUPCAKES

INGREDIENTS
FOR CUPCAKES

1 box white cake mix

3 large eggs

⅔ cup vegetable or canola oil

1¼ cups milk

1 box instant vanilla pudding mix

1 cup brewed coffee, at room temperature

FOR FROSTING & TOPPING

8 tablespoons (1 stick) unsalted butter, at room temperature

¼ cup Kahlúa (or ¼ cup brewed coffee, at room temperature)

1 teaspoon pure vanilla extract

4 cups confectioners' sugar

¼ cup heavy cream

Chocolate syrup and chocolate-covered espresso beans for garnish

1. Prepare the cupcakes: Preheat your oven to 350°F. Line two muffin tins with 18 to 20 paper liners; set aside.

2. Beat together the cake mix, eggs, oil, milk, and vanilla pudding mix in a large bowl, using an electric mixer, until combined and smooth, about 2 minutes. Portion the batter evenly among the prepared muffin cups, filling about three-quarters full.

3. Bake for 15 to 18 minutes, until a toothpick inserted near the center comes out clean or with moist crumbs. Remove from the oven and allow to cool completely. Once cooled, poke holes all over the surface of the cupcake and drizzle each cupcake with a tablespoon or so of coffee. Let the coffee soak into the cupcakes for about 15 minutes.

4. Prepare the frosting: Cream together the butter, Kahlúa (or brewed coffee), and vanilla in a large bowl until smooth, about 2 minutes. Gradually beat in the confectioners' sugar, alternating with the cream, until frosting is light and fluffy.

5. Pipe or spread the frosting onto the cooled cupcakes and garnish with a drizzling of chocolate sauce and top with chocolate-covered espresso beans.

Successful Bars
Tips and Tricks

* I like lining my pans with parchment paper or aluminum foil beforehand. This makes cleanup a breeze, and you can also lift the bars easily out of the pan using "handles" on the sides of the pan made from excess parchment or foil. This makes it a cinch to cut the bars!

* To line a pan, I flip the pan upside down and tear off a piece of foil or parchment larger than the pan. I drape the foil or paper over the bottom of the pan, conforming the foil around the pan's edges and sides. I gently lift off the foil or paper, flip the pan, and then the foil easily slips right into the pan perfectly every time!

* I recommend using cooking spray to spray the foil before adding the bar recipe to the pan.

* My most-used pans are a 9-×-13-inch rectangular baking pan and an 8- or 9-inch square baking pan. I prefer using metal pans as I find they cook more evenly, but if all you have are glass pans, please feel free to use those! If you do use a glass pan, please lower the suggested oven temperature by 25° to account for the different cooking speed of the glass pan.

Blondies, Brownies, and Bars

Bars are my favorite treat to whip up! How can you go wrong with a one-pan treat? In this chapter, you'll find Apple Crisp Bars, Birthday Cake Gooey Bars, and everything in between! Enjoy!

Apple Crisp Bars

Apple crisp (or, let's be honest, any apple dessert!) is my favorite. Nothing feels cozier than a big old plate filled with the gooey stuff. Whether you like it warm or à la mode, there's really no wrong way to eat it. My new favorite way happens to be as a bar. It's almost like a portable pie—a brown sugar shortbread crust topped with cinnamon-spiced apples and an addictive streusel crisp on top. An on-the-go apple crisp? You can thank me later.

9 BARS

INGREDIENTS

FOR CRUST & FILLING

Cooking spray

8 tablespoons (1 stick) unsalted butter, at room temperature

¼ cup brown sugar

¼ cup granulated sugar

1 teaspoon pure vanilla extract

¼ teaspoon salt

1 cup all-purpose flour

One 21-ounce can apple pie filling (see Note)

FOR STREUSEL

8 tablespoons (1 stick) unsalted butter, melted

½ cup brown sugar

½ cup old-fashioned oats

1 teaspoon ground cinnamon

1½ cups all-purpose flour

NOTE: You can substitute the canned pie filling with fresh apples, if preferred. Just peel and dice 4 cups of Granny Smith apples and sauté them with 3 tablespoons brown sugar, 2 teaspoons ground cinnamon, ¼ teaspoon ground nutmeg, and ¼ teaspoon ground ginger, in 2 tablespoons unsalted butter for 5 minutes.

1. Prepare the crust and filling: Preheat your oven to 325°F. Line an 8-inch square baking pan with foil, extending the sides of the foil over the edges of the pan. Spray the foil liberally with cooking spray; set aside.

2. Mix together all the crust ingredients in a medium bowl until moistened and combined. Press in an even layer in the bottom of the prepared pan and bake for 10 minutes. Remove from the oven and increase the oven temperature to 350°F.

3. Pour the apple pie filling evenly over the crust layer.

4. Prepare the streusel: Combine the streusel ingredients in a medium bowl until moistened.

5. Drop heaping handfuls of the streusel topping onto the apple pie filling. Bake for another 30 minutes, or until golden brown on top and set. Remove from the oven and allow to cool completely before cutting into bars.

Peanut Butter and Jelly Bars

One of my favorite snacks as a kid (and, okay, an adult) is a peanut butter and jelly sandwich. I am a fan of grape jelly in mine, but my favorite combination? Apple mint jelly and peanut butter. Before you wrinkle your nose, hear me out. The mint jelly (traditionally served with lamb, which oddly I've never eaten) is surprisingly delicious with the salty peanut butter. However, since I know people will balk at my crazy jelly choices, I've made these with grape jelly. Use strawberry if that's your thing! **16 BARS**

INGREDIENTS

Cooking spray

1 box yellow cake mix

1 large egg

½ cup creamy peanut butter

One 14-ounce can sweetened condensed milk

1 cup grape jelly (or your favorite jelly flavor)

1 cup white chocolate chips

Confectioners' sugar for dusting (optional)

1. Preheat your oven to 350°F. Line a 9-×-13-inch rectangular baking pan with foil, extending the sides of the foil over the edges of the pan. Spray the foil with cooking spray; set aside.

2. Mix together the cake mix, egg, and peanut butter in a medium bowl until blended. Press the dough into the prepared pan in an even layer.

3. Mix together the sweetened condensed milk and grape jelly in a bowl; pour the mixture evenly over the base. Sprinkle with the white chocolate chips.

4. Bake for 22 to 26 minutes, until just about set. If it jiggles a little, that's okay, but it should not be sloshing in the pan. It will continue to set as it cools. Remove from the oven and allow to cool completely, then refrigerate for 2 hours before cutting into bars. Dust with confectioners' sugar before serving.

Muddy Buddy Bars

Muddy buddies are such an addictively easy treat to make, but making them into bars is a totally awesome way to make them portable or perfect for serving a crowd. A fun spin on crispy rice treats, this version is chocolaty, peanut buttery, and submerged in confectioners' sugar for a sweet touch, just like regular muddy buddies. Just try to stop at one!

16 BARS

INGREDIENTS

Cooking spray

¾ cup semisweet chocolate chips

⅓ cup creamy peanut butter

4 tablespoons (½ stick) unsalted butter

3 cups miniature marshmallows

2 cups Cocoa Krispies or similar cereal

2 cups Rice Krispies or similar cereal

2 cups confectioners' sugar

1. Spray a 9-×-13-inch rectangular baking pan with cooking spray. Set aside.

2. Melt together the chocolate chips, peanut butter, butter, and marshmallows in a large saucepan over medium heat, stirring until smooth.

3. Fold in both of the cereals and stir until fully coated. Press into the prepared pan in an even layer and let set for about 1 hour at room temperature.

4. Cut into bars and dredge the bars in the confectioners' sugar until fully coated.

Pecan Pie Gooey Bars

I wasn't the brightest kid, although my parents would disagree, of course.
I say I wasn't bright because I claimed to not like a lot of the foods I love
today, namely pies, of all things. Key Lime, pumpkin, pecan . . . I claimed
to hate them all. When I decided to wake up and smell the pie, I realized
I actually loved all of these pies . . . a lot. I've been making up for lost time
since then. These Pecan Pie Gooey Bars combine the portability of bars with
the gooey pecan pie goodness we all know and love. Little Hayley, this one's
for you. **16 BARS**

INGREDIENTS

FOR CRUST

Cooking spray

1 box yellow cake mix

1 large egg

8 tablespoons (1 stick) unsalted butter,
  melted

FOR FILLING

One 8-ounce package cream cheese,
  at room temperature

3 large eggs

1 teaspoon pure vanilla extract

One 16-ounce box confectioners' sugar

¼ cup dark corn syrup

4 tablespoons (½ stick) unsalted butter,
  melted

1½ cups chopped pecans

1. Prepare the crust: Preheat your oven to 350°F.
Line a 9-×-13-inch rectangular pan with foil,
extending the sides of the foil over the edges of the
pan. Spray the foil with cooking spray.

2. Combine the cake mix, egg, and melted butter in
a large bowl. Press the dough into the prepared pan
in an even layer. Set aside.

3. Prepare the filling: Beat the cream cheese in
a large bowl, using an electric mixer, for about
1 minute or until smooth. Beat in the eggs, one at
a time, until combined. Beat in the vanilla and
confectioners' sugar until smooth. Finally, beat in
the corn syrup and melted butter until combined.
Fold in the pecans.

4. Pour the filling over the crust and bake for
38 to 42 minutes, until just about set. The middle
may still jiggle, but it should not be sloshing around.
Remove from the oven and allow to cool completely,
then refrigerate for at least 2 hours before cutting
into bars.

Crème Brûlée Cheesecake Bars

These Crème Brûlée Cheesecake Bars are a delicious new spin on a family favorite recipe, my Sopapilla Cheesecake Bars. Growing up, we'd often frequent a local restaurant called Coco Loco that served the best sopapillas. Sopapillas are basically fried dough covered in cinnamon sugar, and they're kinda the best thing ever. After making them into a cheesecake bar, I started thinking that the base recipe would be amazing with a crème brûlée twist . . . and here we are! Give these a try and try not to groan in happiness. **16 BARS**

INGREDIENTS

Cooking spray

Two 8-ounce packages refrigerated crescent rolls

Two 8-ounce packages cream cheese, at room temperature

2 teaspoons pure vanilla extract

1½ cups sugar

8 tablespoons (1 stick) unsalted butter, melted

2 teaspoons ground cinnamon

2 cups toffee bits

1. Preheat your oven to 350°F. Spray a 9-×-13-inch rectangular baking pan with cooking spray. Unroll one package of crescent rolls and place the whole sheet in the bottom of the pan, using your fingers to press the perforations together to seal.

2. Beat together the cream cheese, vanilla, and 1 cup of the sugar in a medium bowl, using an electric mixer, for about 1 minute, until smooth. Spread the cheesecake filling on top of the crescent roll sheet, spreading it evenly to the edges.

3. Top with the remaining sheet of crescent roll dough, pinching the perforations together to seal. Pour the melted butter evenly over the top. Whisk together the remaining ½ cup of sugar and the cinnamon in a small bowl until combined; sprinkle over the top. Finally, top with the toffee bits.

4. Bake for 30 to 35 minutes, until the top is golden brown and set. Remove from the oven and allow to cool completely, then refrigerate for at least 2 hours before cutting into squares.

Blondie-Topped Brownies

I am the most indecisive person ever. When faced with life's challenges choices, such as fries or onion rings, the black shirt or the other black shirt, or soup or salad, I seize up under the pressure and make rash decisions that I usually regret later. (Why didn't I get the soup?!) But these Blondie-Topped Brownies are here to end all that fussing once and for all. Now when you're faced with the dilemma of a chewy, brown sugary blondie or a fudgy brownie, you won't have to choose because you can have *both* in one unique bar! 16 BARS

INGREDIENTS

FOR BROWNIES

Cooking spray

1 box fudge brownie mix

2/3 cup vegetable or canola oil

1 large egg

FOR BLONDIES

16 tablespoons (2 sticks) unsalted butter

2 cups brown sugar

2 large eggs

1 tablespoon pure vanilla extract

1 teaspoon baking soda

½ teaspoon salt

2 cups all-purpose flour

1. Prepare the brownies: Preheat your oven to 350°F. Line a 9-×-13-inch rectangular baking pan with foil, extending the sides of the foil over the edges of the pan. Spray the foil liberally with cooking spray.

2. Combine the brownie mix, oil, and egg in a large bowl until blended. Press the dough in the bottom of the pan in an even layer. Set aside.

3. Prepare the blondies: Melt the butter in a large saucepan over medium heat. Turn off the heat once the butter has melted and whisk in the brown sugar. Add the eggs, one at a time, mixing well after each addition, followed by the vanilla. Whisk in the baking soda, salt, and flour until a thick batter forms.

4. Spread the blondie batter over the brownie base in an even layer. Bake for 40 to 45 minutes, until the top is golden brown and a toothpick inserted near the center comes out clean or with moist crumbs. Remove from the oven and allow to cool completely before cutting into bars.

Cinnamon Roll Blondies

Cinnamon rolls have to be one of my favorite foods in the world. Anytime I'm near a pan, I just have to have it, even if I just ate a big meal. You just can't go wrong with a big, fluffy yeast roll stuffed to the gills with cinnamon sugar and butter. And the frosting is just the icing on the cake. Or roll. Whatever. When I set out to create this book, I knew I had to cinnamon roll-ify something, and it just so happened to be these blondies. These bars are not for the cinnamon faint-of-heart, but if you could eat cinnamon by the pound like me, you'll love these! 16 BARS

INGREDIENTS

FOR BLONDIES

Cooking spray

16 tablespoons (2 sticks) unsalted butter

2 cups brown sugar

2 large eggs

1 tablespoon pure vanilla extract

1 tablespoon ground cinnamon

1 teaspoon baking soda

½ teaspoon salt

2 cups all-purpose flour

FOR FROSTING

2 tablespoons unsalted butter, at room temperature

4 ounces cream cheese, at room temperature

1 teaspoon pure vanilla extract

1½ cups confectioners' sugar

2 to 3 tablespoons heavy cream or milk

1. Prepare the blondies: Preheat your oven to 350°F. Spray a 9-×-13-inch rectangular baking pan with cooking spray; set aside.

2. Melt the butter in a large saucepan over medium heat. Whisk in the brown sugar until combined. Whisk in the eggs, one at a time, followed by the vanilla. Whisk in the cinnamon, baking soda, salt, and flour until a thick batter has formed.

3. Spread the blondie batter in the prepared pan in an even layer and bake for 20 to 22 minutes, until a toothpick inserted near the center comes out clean or with moist crumbs. Remove from the oven and allow to cool completely.

4. Prepare the frosting: Beat together the butter, cream cheese, and vanilla in a medium bowl, using an electric mixer, until combined. Beat in the confectioners' sugar and cream until a fluffy, spreadable frosting has been achieved.

5. Spread the frosting evenly over the blondies and refrigerate for at least 1 hour to set before cutting into bars.

Strawberry Shortcake Bars

These Strawberry Shortcake Bars remind me of a garden party where everyone serves tea and cucumber sandwiches. Or, at least, what I imagine garden parties would be like. If anyone wants to invite me to one, that'd be awesome and I'll totally bring these bars. The best part is, they could not be easier to make, so you have more time to drink tea and play croquet, or whatever people do at garden parties. Simply a sugar cookie base topped with a luscious cream cheese icing and fresh strawberries. I'll be waiting for my invite! 16 BARS

INGREDIENTS

Cooking spray

Two 16.5-ounce packages refrigerated sugar cookie dough, at room temperature

One 8-ounce package cream cheese, at room temperature

¼ cup sugar

1 teaspoon pure vanilla extract

One 8-ounce tub frozen whipped topping, such as Cool Whip, thawed

2 pints fresh strawberries, sliced

1. Preheat your oven to 350°F. Line a 9-×-13-inch rectangular baking pan with foil, extending the foil over the edges of the pan. Spray the foil liberally with cooking spray.

2. Tear off chunks of the cookie dough and gently flatten them in the palm of your hand. Press them into the pan, almost like doing a jigsaw puzzle, until the cookie dough is in an even layer. Bake for 25 to 28 minutes, until light golden brown and set. Remove from the oven and allow to cool completely.

3. Beat together the cream cheese, sugar, and vanilla in a large bowl, using an electric mixer, until creamy, about 1 minute. Fold in the whipped topping until fluffy and combined.

4. Spread the cream cheese mixture over the top of the baked dough and top with the sliced strawberries. Refrigerate until set, about 2 hours, before cutting into bars.

French Silk Pie Brownies

Sometimes as a kid, we'd go to a restaurant that's known for their famous pies. My family and I would practically scarf down our dinner so we could get straight to the pie-eating part of the meal. My favorite pie switched depending on the day of the week but usually came back to loving apple. However, once I tried French silk pie, it was kind of a close call. Normally I'm not a big chocolate person, but I loved how light and fluffy the French silk filling was. That filling is exactly what tops these moist and fudgy brownies . . . and makes it a new contender for favorite pie! 16 BROWNIES

INGREDIENTS

FOR BROWNIES

1 box fudge brownie mix

¼ cup water

½ cup vegetable or canola oil

2 large eggs

FOR TOPPING

One 4-ounce German chocolate bar, finely chopped

4 tablespoons (½ stick) unsalted butter, cubed

One 8-ounce package cream cheese, at room temperature

2 cups confectioners' sugar

One 16-ounce tub frozen whipped topping, such as Cool Whip, thawed

Chocolate curls, for decorating (optional)

1. Prepare and bake the brownies according to the package directions. Remove from the oven and allow to cool completely.

2. Microwave the German chocolate pieces and butter together in a large microwave-safe bowl on HIGH for 30 seconds. Stir, and then melt for another 15 seconds. Stir until smooth and melted.

3. Beat in the cream cheese and confectioners' sugar until combined. Fold in half of the whipped topping (8 ounces).

4. Spread the French silk filling over the brownies. Top with the remaining whipped topping and garnish with chocolate curls, if using.

5. Refrigerate for at least 4 hours, or until set, before cutting into squares.

Birthday Cake Gooey Bars

My parents never baked for us kids when we were growing up, but if we begged them hard enough, they'd eventually supervise us while we baked our own cake. And without fail, we always chose the confetti cake mix. Is it just me, or is the confetti cake mix clearly the superior of all the mixes? It's always so moist and fluffy and you cannot go wrong with sprinkles. These Birthday Cake Gooey Bars are inspired by all the confetti cakes I'd make as a kid . . . and all the gooey bars I eat as an adult! **16 BARS**

INGREDIENTS

FOR CRUST

Cooking spray

1 box confetti cake mix

1 large egg

8 tablespoons (1 stick) unsalted butter, melted

FOR FILLING

One 8-ounce package cream cheese, at room temperature

3 large eggs

One 16-ounce box confectioners' sugar

1 teaspoon pure vanilla extract

½ teaspoon almond extract

4 tablespoons (1 stick) unsalted butter, melted

1 cup rainbow sprinkles

1. Prepare the crust: Preheat your oven to 350°F. Line a 9-×-13-inch rectangular baking pan with foil, extending the sides of the foil over the edges of the pan. Spray liberally with cooking spray.

2. Mix together the crust ingredients in a medium bowl until moistened. Press the dough evenly in the bottom of the pan. Set aside.

3. Prepare the filling: Cream the cream cheese in a large bowl, using an electric mixer, about 1 minute. Beat in the eggs, one at a time, followed by the confectioners' sugar and vanilla and almond extracts. Stream in the melted butter until combined, then fold in the rainbow sprinkles.

4. Pour the filling mixture evenly over the crust and bake for 38 to 42 minutes, until the top is mostly set. The center may jiggle a little, but it should not be sloshing in the pan. Remove from the oven and allow to cool completely, then refrigerate for at least 4 hours until set before cutting into bars.

Texas Sheet Cake Brownies

I'm a California girl born and raised, but I lament the fact that Californians don't have cakes the size of Texas. Sure, California has a bounty of fruits and vegetables, but choosing between an avocado and a chocolate cake is a no-brainer. If you haven't tried Texas sheet cake before, it's a must-try. And if you haven't tried Texas Sheet Cake Brownies before, you better be heading to the kitchen to whip up a pan STAT. I'll trade you an avocado for a slice! 16 BROWNIES

INGREDIENTS

FOR BROWNIES

1 box fudge brownie mix

¼ cup water

½ cup vegetable or canola oil

2 large eggs

FOR TOPPING

8 tablespoons (1 stick) unsalted butter

5 tablespoons unsweetened cocoa powder

6 tablespoons milk

4 cups confectioners' sugar

1 teaspoon pure vanilla extract

1 cup chopped pecans

1. Prepare and bake the brownies according to the package directions. Remove from the oven and allow to cool completely.

2. Melt together the butter, cocoa powder, and milk in a medium saucepan over medium heat, stirring constantly. Whisk in the confectioners' sugar one cup at a time, followed by the vanilla. Fold in the chopped pecans.

3. Pour the frosting over the brownie layer and let set, about 1 hour, before cutting into squares.

Peanut Butter Cup Bars

If you are a fan of peanut butter cups (and really, who isn't?), you have got to give these bars a try. If you've ever wanted a peanut butter cup to be humongous, you have got to give these bars a try. If you've ever wanted the peanut butter filling ratio to be a little bigger, thicker, more in-your-face, you have got to give these bars a try! What I'm trying to say is, you have to try these! Unless you don't like peanut butter . . . in which case, I'll see you on the next page! **16 BARS**

INGREDIENTS

FOR CRUST

16 tablespoons (2 sticks) unsalted butter, melted

2 cups graham cracker crumbs

2 cups confectioners' sugar

1 cup creamy peanut butter

FOR TOPPING

2 cups semisweet chocolate chips

¼ cup creamy peanut butter

1. Line a 9-×-13-inch rectangular baking pan with parchment paper, extending the sides of the parchment over the edges of the pan. Set aside.

2. Stir together the melted butter, graham cracker crumbs, confectioners' sugar, and 1 cup of the peanut butter in a large bowl until blended and smooth.

3. Press the peanut butter mixture into the prepared pan. Refrigerate for at least 30 minutes.

4. Microwave the chocolate chips with the remaining ¼ cup of peanut butter in a medium microwave-safe bowl on HIGH for 30 seconds. Stir, then microwave again for another 10 to 15 seconds. Stir until melted and smooth.

5. Pour the chocolate mixture evenly over the peanut butter layer and smooth out the surface. Refrigerate for at least 4 hours or until completely set before cutting into bars.

Chocolate Caramel Candy Cookie Bars

You know when you're buying Halloween candy and you obviously buy a bag filled with candy you like, because what if an apocalypse happens and no kids show up? But inevitably, there's a candy in that bag that you're kind of so-so with? You don't hate it, but it will be the leavings when you're finished with the rest? That's how I felt about Twix . . . until this year. Then I tried one out of desperation and it was like a whole new world opened up for me. I could finally see the beauty in the world . . . and in the candy, too. So, you bet your bottom dollar that for this book I was making recipe to use up that candy, and here she is! Say good-bye to being picked last, Twix!

16 BARS

INGREDIENTS

Cooking spray

Two 16.5-ounce packages refrigerated sugar cookie dough, at room temperature

One 11-ounce bag caramel bits (or square caramels)

¾ cup heavy cream or milk

2 cups semisweet chocolate chips

1. Preheat your oven to 350°F. Line a 9-×-13-inch rectangular baking pan with foil, extending the foil over the edges of the pan. Spray the foil liberally with cooking spray.

2. Tear off chunks of the cookie dough and gently flatten them in the palm of your hand. Press them into the pan, almost like doing a jigsaw puzzle, until the cookie dough is in an even layer. Bake for 25 to 30 minutes, until light golden brown and set. Remove from the oven and allow to cool completely.

3. Melt the caramel bits with ¼ cup of the cream in a medium saucepan over medium-low heat, stirring constantly until smooth. Pour the caramel mixture evenly over the bars and gently spread to the edges in an even layer. Refrigerate for about 1 hour.

4. Microwave the chocolate chips with the remaining ½ cup of cream in a medium microwave-safe bowl on HIGH for 30 seconds. Stir, then microwave for an additional 10 to 15 seconds. Stir until melted. Pour the melted chocolate over the caramel layer, smoothing to the edges in an even layer. Refrigerate for at least 2 hours or until set before cutting into bars.

Sugar Cookie Cheesecake Bars

Sugar cookies are a must-have in the Parker household. Because of my blog and crazy baking schedule, I don't make them nearly as often as I'd like to, so when I do, they're the first to go. I got the idea for these Sugar Cookie Cheesecake Bars because we also like cheesecake in this house, and who doesn't love a fun mash-up requiring creamy cheesecake and sweet sugar cookies?! 9 BARS

INGREDIENTS

FOR CRUST

Cooking spray

24 Birthday Cake Golden Oreo or similar cookies

4 tablespoons (½ stick) unsalted butter, melted

FOR FILLING & TOPPING

Two 8-ounce packages cream cheese, at room temperature

⅔ cup sugar

2 large eggs

1 tablespoon pure vanilla extract

½ teaspoon almond extract

⅓ cup sour cream

Whipped cream, sprinkles, and additional cookies for garnish

1. Prepare the crust: Preheat your oven to 325°F. Line an 8-inch square baking pan with foil, extending the sides of the foil over the edges of the pan. Spray the foil liberally with cooking spray.

2. Crush the cookies into fine crumbs and mix with the melted butter until moistened. Press the cookie mixture into the bottom of the prepared pan, pressing it gently in an even layer. Bake for 12 minutes.

3. Prepare the filling: Beat together the cream cheese and sugar in a large bowl, using an electric mixer on medium speed, until creamy, about 2 minutes. Beat in the eggs, one at a time, beating well after each addition, followed by the vanilla and almond extracts. Finally, beat in the sour cream to combine.

4. Pour the cheesecake filling into the prepared pan and smooth out the top. Bake for 35 to 40 minutes, until the top is light golden brown and the center is just about set. If it jiggles a little, that's okay, but it should not be sloshing around in the pan. Remove from the oven and allow to cool completely, then refrigerate for at least 4 hours before cutting into bars. Just before serving, top with whipped cream, sprinkles, and a cookie half.

Successful Pie and Cheesecake
Tips and Tricks

* I recommend placing your pie pans on a rimmed baking sheet during baking to prevent spillovers that may happen from the pie. Bonus: If you foil-line the rimmed baking sheet, there's one less dish to wash!

* To make it easier on you and me, I used prepared piecrusts in these recipes, whether that is graham cracker or refrigerated pie dough. If you prefer a scratch-made recipe, feel free to substitute that.

* For most baked pies, I recommend allowing them to cool completely before cutting into slices. For frozen or refrigerated pies, it is okay to cut straight from the fridge or freezer.

* For all my pie recipes, I cannot live without piecrust shields. These are either flexible tools you piece together to form a circle around the crust, or a circular single piece you place over the crust. This prevents the crust from browning too quickly but still allows the filling to bake properly. If you don't have these tools, simply use strips of aluminum foil to gently tent the crust.

4

Pies and Cheesecakes

French Silk Cookie Pies

Cookies are all fine and dandy, but have you thought about turning cookies into pies?! Bite-size morsels of heaven that are filled with a chocolaty silk filling nestled in a cookie crust. This is the real deal, people! Welcome to the new world of eating pie. 24 COOKIE PIES

INGREDIENTS

Cooking spray

One 16.5-ounce package (24-count) refrigerated chocolate chip cookie dough

2 ounces German chocolate, roughly chopped

4 ounces cream cheese, at room temperature

¾ cup confectioners' sugar

12 ounces frozen whipped topping, such as Cool Whip, thawed

Chocolate shavings for garnish (optional)

1. Preheat your oven to 350°F. Liberally spray a 24-cavity miniature muffin pan with cooking spray. Place one cookie dough ball in each muffin cavity and use your fingers to gently press down on the cookie dough. Bake for 10 to 12 minutes, until golden brown and the centers appear set. Remove from the oven and allow to cool for 15 minutes, then use the handle of a wooden spoon to make an indentation in the center of each cookie cup and allow to cool completely.

2. Microwave the chocolate in a medium microwave-safe bowl on HIGH for 20 seconds. Stir until melted and smooth. Add the cream cheese and confectioners' sugar to the bowl and beat with an electric mixer until fluffy, about 2 minutes. Fold in 1 cup of the whipped topping until fluffy.

3. Pipe the French silk filling into each cookie cup, or use a tablespoon to dollop the filling into each cookie cup. Top with a dollop or a small piping's worth of the remaining whipped topping, then garnish with chocolate shavings, if using.

Berry Cherry Cobbler Pie

Growing up, we didn't eat a lot of cobblers or crisps. In fact, we never ate them and I wasn't aware of what they were, exactly, until we'd see them at a restaurant and I'd beg my parents to let me order one. Now, if I see a cobbler on the menu, it's almost always ordered because who can resist that bubbly, sugary, biscuit-y topping? Certainly not me! This pie combines a berry cherry pie with a cobbler topping for an irresistible mash-up you just have to try! Don't like berries? Use all cherry or substitute for peach or apple.

8 SLICES

INGREDIENTS

Cooking spray

1 refrigerated piecrust, at room temperature

One 21-ounce can mixed berry pie filling (or 2 cups fresh or thawed frozen berries)

One 21-ounce can cherry pie filling (see Note)

¼ cup granulated sugar

¼ cup brown sugar

1 cup all-purpose flour

1 teaspoon baking powder

5 tablespoons unsalted butter, cubed

¼ cup milk

1 large egg, lightly beaten

NOTE: You can substitute the canned cherry pie filling with 2 cups pitted fresh or thawed frozen cherries tossed with ⅔ cup granulated sugar.

1. Preheat your oven to 350°F. Lightly spray a 9-inch-diameter pie plate with cooking spray. Drape the piecrust over the pie plate and gently press the crust into the plate. Crimp or tuck in the piecrust's edges and fill the crust with both pie fillings, using a spoon to gently mix them together in the crust. Set aside.

2. Whisk together the sugars, flour, and baking powder in a medium bowl. Cut in the butter, using two forks or a pastry cutter, until the mixture resembles coarse crumbs. Add the milk and beaten egg and gently mix to combine. Do not overmix, as this leads to a tough cobbler topping; the mixture should just barely come together.

3. Drop heaping spoonfuls of the cobbler mixture evenly over the pie. Bake for 50 to 65 minutes, until the cobbler topping is light golden brown and bubbly. You may need to tent the top of the pie with foil if the cobbler is browning too quickly; check at the halfway mark. Remove the pie from the oven and allow to cool to room temperature. Serve with ice cream, if desired.

Deep-Dish Chocolate Chip Cookie Tart

When I first had a deep-dish cookie, it was like magic. You know the moment right before someone starts an impromptu dance sequence in a movie? I felt like that person in that moment. This one is extra-special, because it's filled with chocolate ganache, which is what I want to bathe in when I'm rich and famous. It also has frosting, so there's a little extra oomph on top. If you don't break out into song and dance after taking a bite, take another bite and try not to do the Lindy Hop afterward. **12–14 SLICES**

INGREDIENTS

FOR COOKIE

Cooking spray

12 tablespoons (1½ sticks) unsalted butter, at room temperature

1 cup brown sugar

½ cup granulated sugar

1 large egg

1 large egg yolk

1 tablespoon pure vanilla extract

1 teaspoon baking soda

1 teaspoon cornstarch

½ teaspoon salt

2 cups all-purpose flour

1½ cups semisweet chocolate chips

FOR GANACHE & FROSTING

1 cup semisweet chocolate chips

⅓ cup plus ¼ cup heavy cream

4 tablespoons (½ stick) unsalted butter

1 teaspoon pure vanilla extract

1½ cups confectioners' sugar

Chocolate sprinkles for garnish (optional)

1. Preheat your oven to 350°F. Liberally spray a 9- or 10-inch-diameter round tart pan with cooking spray. Place on a baking sheet to make it easier to transfer in and out of the oven. Set aside.

2. Cream together the butter, brown sugar, and granulated sugar in a large bowl, using an electric mixer on medium speed, about 2 minutes. Beat in the egg, egg yolk, and vanilla until blended. Finally, beat in the baking soda, cornstarch, salt, and flour until a soft dough forms. Fold in the chocolate chips.

3. Press the cookie dough into the tart pan in an even layer. Bake for 25 to 30 minutes, until golden brown and the center appears mostly set. It's okay if the center jiggles a little, but it should not be sloshing around in the pan. Remove from the oven and allow to cool completely.

4. Prepare the ganache: Microwave the chocolate chips and ⅓ cup of the cream in a medium microwave-safe bowl on HIGH for 30 seconds. Stir, then melt for another 10 to 15 seconds, until melted and smooth. Pour the ganache over the cookie tart and spread to the edges. Let set for 20 minutes.

5. Prepare the frosting: Beat together the butter, vanilla, ¼ cup of cream, and the confectioners' sugar in a medium bowl until light and fluffy. Pipe the frosting onto the edges of the cookie tart.

Fudge Brownie Pie

Did you know you can bake almost anything into a piecrust? Why should traditional pie filling have all the fun? This chapter should have already showed you that you can create classic desserts and transform them into gooey, outrageously awesome pies . . . and this Fudge Brownie Pie is no exception! Personally, I love this topped with a big scoop of vanilla ice cream and a drizzling of chocolate sauce, but top it with whatever your heart wants. **8–10 SLICES**

INGREDIENTS

Cooking spray

1 refrigerated piecrust, at room temperature

One 15.25-ounce package brownie mix (for an 8-inch square pan), plus ingredients listed on back of package (see Note)

1 cup semisweet chocolate chips

Ice cream, whipped cream, or desired toppings (optional)

NOTE: I'm calling for the smaller box of mix here, but you can use a family size brownie mix (about 18 ounces), too. You may have a little batter left. If so, bake it off in a ramekin!

1. Preheat your oven to 350°F. Lightly spray a 9-inch round pie plate with cooking spray. Drape the piecrust over the pie plate and gently press the crust into the plate. Crimp or tuck in the piecrust edges and sprinkle the bottom of the piecrust with the chocolate chips.

2. Prepare the brownie mix according to the package instructions; pour the brownie batter into the piecrust to about half an inch from top and smooth out the top.

3. Bake for 25 to 30 minutes, until the top is set and a toothpick inserted near the center comes out clean or with moist crumbs. Remove from the oven and allow to cool completely before cutting into slices. Serve with ice cream, whipped cream, chocolate sauce, or your desired toppings.

Tiramisu Pie

One of my favorite desserts to order at a restaurant would be tiramisu. I just adore the stuff, mostly because it's unlike anything I ever grew up eating. There is something to be said about the combination of coffee, chocolate, and that luscious creamy mascarpone filling. It's truly remarkable! Truthfully, I've never made an actual tiramisu from scratch; in my neck of the woods, ladyfingers aren't easy to come by. But pound cake is and it makes a fabulous substitute for this amazing pie! 8–10 SLICES

INGREDIENTS

1 Oreo or similar cookie piecrust

Five ¼-inch slices prepared pound cake

2 tablespoons brewed coffee

One 8-ounce package whipped cream cheese

¼ cup confectioners' sugar

1 teaspoon pure vanilla extract

½ cup chocolate syrup

One 8-ounce tub frozen whipped topping, such as Cool Whip, thawed

Additional whipped cream and chocolate shavings (optional but recommended)

1. Place the pound cake pieces flat in the bottom of the piecrust, cutting the pieces, if necessary, to fit. Drizzle the pound cake pieces with the coffee; set aside.

2. Whip together the whipped cream cheese, confectioners' sugar, and vanilla in a large bowl, using an electric mixer, until creamy, about 2 minutes. Beat in the chocolate syrup until combined, then fold in the whipped topping until fluffy and light.

3. Spread the cream cheese mixture over the pound cake in the prepared piecrust and smooth out the top. Refrigerate for at least 6 to 8 hours, until firm and set, before cutting into slices. If desired, garnish with whipped cream and chocolate shavings just before serving.

Creamy Orange Soda Pie

This pie tastes just like summertime in one frosty, chilly treat. The best part? It's entirely no-bake, so when you're in the heat of the summer and the idea of turning on the oven sounds worse than going to the dentist, this pie will be your savior. It comes together in minutes, although it does need to chill, so I recommend making it the night before you need to serve it, or first thing in the morning so it'll be ready for you at the end of the day. Make it, eat it, love it! **8–10 SLICES**

INGREDIENTS

¾ cup orange soda

½ cup milk

1 box instant vanilla pudding mix

Zest of 1 orange

2 teaspoons fresh orange juice or orange extract

One 8-ounce tub frozen whipped topping, such as Cool Whip, thawed

One 9-inch graham cracker crust

Additional whipped cream for serving (optional)

1. Whisk together the orange soda, milk, vanilla pudding mix, orange zest, and orange juice or extract in a large bowl until combined and thickened, about 2 minutes. Fold in the whipped topping until uniform in color and fluffy in texture.

2. Pour the filling into the prepared graham cracker crust and freeze for 8 hours, preferably overnight, before cutting into slices to serve. This pie is best served straight from the freezer. Serve with whipped cream on the side, if desired.

Cannoli Pie

When I first visited New York City, I was on strict order to try an authentic Italian cannoli. And when I did, it was like the skies parted and angels sang, because it was marvelous and a total texture explosion. Crunchy shell, creamy filling, a little pop from chocolate chips . . . total heaven! Those classic Italian cannoli are what inspired me to make this pie, which is a lot easier to whip up and is just as fabulous. 8–10 SLICES

INGREDIENTS

One 9-inch store-bought or homemade chocolate cookie crust

1 cup ricotta cheese

2/3 cup sugar

1 teaspoon pure vanilla extract

One 8-ounce tub frozen whipped topping, such as Cool Whip, thawed

1½ cups miniature chocolate chips

1 cup coarsely crushed waffle cookies

1. Beat together the ricotta cheese, sugar, and vanilla in a large bowl, using an electric mixer, until creamy and blended, about 1 minute. Fold in the whipped topping until light and fluffy. Toss in 1 cup of the miniature chocolate chips and fold to combine.

2. Pour the mixture into the prepared crust and smooth out the top. Top with the remaining chocolate chips and the crushed waffle cookies. Freeze for at least 4 to 6 hours, until firm.

Pecan Pie Cheesecake Pie

Pecan pie is already a sight for sore eyes. Gooey, crunchy, and totally perfect for any occasion, it's one of my dad's favorite pies. But sometimes pecan pie leaves little to the imagination, am I right? I mean, it's kind of predictable and needs a little *je ne sais quoi* at times. Enter: this Pecan Pie Cheesecake Pie. It is a regular pecan pie's rock star cousin. A little loud, a little in-your-face, and a whole lotta flavor and attitude. And dare I say, even better than the original? 8–10 SLICES

INGREDIENTS

FOR CHEESECAKE

Cooking spray

1 refrigerated piecrust, at room temperature

One 8-ounce package cream cheese, at room temperature

¼ cup granulated sugar

1 large egg

1 teaspoon pure vanilla extract

FOR TOPPING

2 large eggs

½ cup dark corn syrup

½ cup brown sugar

1 teaspoon pure vanilla extract

1 tablespoon bourbon

3 tablespoons unsalted butter, melted

¼ teaspoon salt

2 cups pecan halves

NOTE: You may need to tent foil around the edges of the piecrust during the baking time (check at the halfway point) to prevent them from burning. A piecrust shield or strips of foil should do the trick.

1. Prepare the cheesecake: Preheat your oven to 350°F. Lightly spray a 9-inch-diameter pie plate with cooking spray. Drape the piecrust evenly over the pie plate and gently press into the plate. Crimp or tuck in the edges of the piecrust. Set aside.

2. Beat together the cream cheese, sugar, egg, and vanilla in a medium bowl, using an electric mixer, until creamy and smooth, about 2 minutes. Pour the cheesecake mixture into the bottom of the crust and smooth out the top. Set aside.

3. Prepare the topping: Whisk together the eggs, corn syrup, brown sugar, vanilla, bourbon, melted butter, and salt in a medium bowl until smooth and blended. Fold in the pecan halves. Pour the mixture evenly over the cheesecake layer.

4. Bake for 35 to 40 minutes, until the center is just about set. If it jiggles a little, that's okay, but it should not be sloshing around in the pan. Remove from the oven and allow to cool completely, then refrigerate for at least 3 hours to set before cutting into slices.

Chocolate Mocha Pie

One of my childhood memories is going to the local coffee shop with my mom and ordering mochas. As a kid, it was so cool to be able to order my own drink at a fancy adult coffee shop . . . and a mocha, no less! I would always order it with extra whipped cream, because you only live once, right? And in the summertime, I always ordered my mochas frozen and icy, which is how I prefer them to this day . . . and especially in pie form!

8–10 SLICES

INGREDIENTS

¾ cup cold-brew coffee

½ cup chocolate milk

1 box instant chocolate pudding mix

One 8-ounce tub frozen whipped topping, such as Cool Whip, thawed

One 9-inch chocolate cookie crust

Additional whipped cream and chocolate syrup for garnish (optional but recommended)

1. Whisk together the coffee, chocolate milk, and chocolate pudding mix in a large bowl until combined and thickened, about 2 minutes. Fold in the whipped topping until uniform in color and fluffy in texture.

2. Pour the filling into the prepared chocolate cookie crust and freeze for 8 hours, preferably overnight, before cutting into slices to serve. This pie is best served straight from the freezer. Serve with whipped cream and chocolate syrup on top, if desired.

Baklava Pie

I remember the first time I tried baklava. It was at a Greek food festival in Sacramento and I thought it was incredible. Soaked with honey, filled with nuts, and layered with crispy phyllo dough, it truly was unlike any other dessert I'd ever tasted. Sadly, I don't make baklava often (it is a little labor-intensive, if you haven't tried before), but I crave it every once in a while and have to make this pie as a way to fix my cravings. Buttery, flaky piecrust filled with gooey, syrupy nuts. Yum! 8–10 SLICES

INGREDIENTS

One package (2-count) refrigerated piecrusts, at room temperature

8 tablespoons (1 stick) unsalted butter, melted

3 cups finely chopped walnuts

½ cup brown sugar

1 teaspoon ground cinnamon

¾ cup honey

1 tablespoon fresh lemon juice

1. Preheat your oven to 325°F. Lightly spray a 9-inch-diameter pie plate with cooking spray. Drape one piecrust evenly over the top of the pie plate and press the crust gently into the plate. Drizzle half of the melted butter into the bottom of the piecrust.

2. Mix together the walnuts, brown sugar, and cinnamon in a bowl until combined. Pour the walnuts into the piecrust; top with the remaining melted butter. Drape the second piecrust on top of the walnut mixture and press the edges of the top and bottom crusts together. Crimp or tuck in the edges of the piecrust. Cut several slits in the top crust, using a knife.

3. Bake for 45 to 55 minutes, until the top is light golden brown. Five to 10 minutes before the pie is finished baking, heat the honey and lemon juice together in a saucepan over medium heat, stirring constantly, until combined, hot, and watery in consistency.

4. Remove the fully baked pie from the oven and immediately pour the hot honey mixture evenly over the pie. Allow to cool completely. Allow to set for at least 2 to 3 hours before cutting into slices.

Snickerdoodle Capookie (Cake/Pie/Cookie)

I know what you're thinking: what in the world is a "capookie"? Let me tell you, but let me also warn you that you'll want capookies from this point forward. A capookie, as I lovingly call it, is a hybrid dessert combining cake, pie, and cookies into one unbelievable monster dessert. And this Snickerdoodle Capookie is the perfect introduction to this new term. It has the flavor of a snickerdoodle cookie, the light and fluffy texture of a piece of cake, and it's baked into a piecrust. Go ahead and pinch yourself, but I promise you're not dreaming! **8–10 SLICES**

INGREDIENTS

4 tablespoons (½ stick) unsalted butter, at room temperature

½ cup granulated sugar

½ cup confectioners' sugar

1 teaspoon baking powder

2 teaspoons ground cinnamon

¼ teaspoon salt

¼ teaspoon cream of tartar

1 large egg

1 teaspoon pure vanilla extract

½ cup milk

1½ cups all-purpose flour

One 9-inch deep-dish frozen piecrust (see Note)

Additional cinnamon sugar and ice cream for serving (optional)

NOTE: I recommend using a deep-dish crust because a regular crust cannot accommodate all of the filling. If you only have a regular-size crust on hand, fill the crust with the filling just about to the top rim of the crust and eat the remaining filling!

1. Preheat your oven to 350°F.

2. Cream together the butter, granulated sugar, and confectioners' sugar in a medium bowl, using an electric mixer on medium speed, about 1 minute. Beat in the baking powder, salt, cinnamon, cream of tartar, egg, and vanilla until combined. Stream in ¼ cup of the milk, beating well, followed by ¾ cup of the flour, beating well. Repeat with remaining ¼ cup of milk first, followed by the remaining ¾ cup of flour.

3. Spread the batter into the piecrust and smooth out the top. Bake for 30 to 40 minutes, until a toothpick inserted near the center comes out clean. Remove from the oven and allow to cool completely before cutting into slices. Serve with ice cream and additional cinnamon sugar, if desired.

Billionaire Cheesecake Pie

No, you do not have to be a billionaire to enjoy this pie, but if you are a billionaire and you're reading this, hi! Can we be friends? Anyway, billionaire bars are big in the blog world and they basically consist of a cookie crust, a layer of caramel, and a layer of cookie dough, topped with chocolate. They are not diet-friendly and they are not shy about being off-the-charts sweet, either. But they are fantastically delicious, and they were the inspiration for this pie! Loaded with cookie dough and topped with caramel and chocolate, it's a force to be reckoned with! **8–10 SLICES**

INGREDIENTS

Two 8-ounce packages cream cheese, at room temperature

²⁄₃ cup sugar

2 large eggs

1 tablespoon pure vanilla extract

¼ cup sour cream

½ (16.5-ounce) tube refrigerated chocolate chip cookie dough (see Note)

One 9-inch store-bought or homemade chocolate cookie crust

1 cup jarred caramel sauce

1 cup semisweet chocolate chips

¼ cup heavy cream

NOTE: Use any leftover cookie dough from the package to bake cookies as a garnish for this recipe!

1. Preheat your oven to 325°F. Cream together the cream cheese and sugar in a large bowl until creamy and smooth, about 2 minutes. Beat in the eggs, one at a time, beating well after each addition, followed by the vanilla. Beat in the sour cream until combined and smooth.

2. Tear off pieces of the cookie dough tube and roll into balls 1 to 2 teaspoons in size. Cover the bottom of the prepared cookie crust with balls of cookie dough; top with half of the cheesecake mixture. Top with another layer of cookie dough balls, followed by the remaining cheesecake mixture.

3. Bake for 40 to 50 minutes, until the top is light golden brown and the center is just about set. If it jiggles a little, that's okay, but it should not be sloshing around in the pan. Remove from the oven and allow to cool completely, then pour on the caramel sauce and spread it out to the edges. Refrigerate for at least an hour.

4. Microwave the chocolate chips and cream together in a medium microwave-safe bowl on HIGH for 25 seconds. Stir, then microwave again for 10 to 15 seconds. Stir until smooth and melted. Pour over the top of the caramel layer and smooth out to the edges. Refrigerate for 30 minutes to set before cutting into slices to serve.

Crème Brûlée Pie

I have a recipe similar to this one on my website called Sugar Cream Pie. When I first discovered Sugar Cream Pie, I had no idea what I was in for . . . but one bite and the rest was history. To this day, it's in my dad's top three favorite desserts *ever*, and if you know him, that's saying something! I wanted to remix the recipe for Sugar Pie and jazz it up a little with more of a crème brûlée flavor, and this is it! If you haven't made homemade crème brûlée out of fear, fear no longer because this pie is even simpler (and *psst*, tastes even better!). 10–12 SLICES

INGREDIENTS

One 9-inch deep-dish frozen piecrust (see Note)

¼ cup cornstarch

¾ cup plus ⅓ cup sugar

8 tablespoons (1 stick) unsalted butter, melted

2¼ cups heavy cream

1 tablespoon vanilla bean paste

1 teaspoon ground cinnamon (optional)

NOTE: I recommend using a deep-dish crust because a regular crust cannot accommodate all of the filling. If you only have a regular-size crust on hand, fill the crust with the filling just about to the top rim of the crust and eat the remaining filling!

1. Preheat your oven to 325°F. Place the deep-dish piecrust on a rimmed baking sheet to catch any spills while baking. Set aside.

2. Whisk together the cornstarch and ¾ cup of the sugar in a medium saucepot until combined. Add 4 tablespoons of the melted butter and the cream and whisk to combine over medium-low heat. Continue to whisk constantly until mixture becomes thick and custardlike, 5 to 7 minutes, keeping a close eye on it so it does not burn. Remove from the heat and immediately whisk in the vanilla bean paste.

3. Pour the filling mixture into the piecrust and smooth out the top. Pour the remaining 4 tablespoons of melted butter over the top and sprinkle with the remaining ⅓ cup of sugar and the cinnamon, if using.

4. Bake for 25 to 30 minutes, until bubbly, golden brown on top and the center is just about set. If it jiggles slightly, that's okay, but it should not be sloshing around in the pan. Remove from the oven and allow to cool completely, then refrigerate for at least 3 hours to set before cutting into slices.

Strawberry Pretzel Salad Pie

When I tried strawberry pretzel salad for the first time, I wondered why I'd not been exposed to it sooner! It's the epitome of summertime to me: fresh, cool, breezy, and easy. The combination of salty, crunchy pretzels, the smooth, creamy filling, and the juicy strawberries just cannot be beat. I have to say, of the 100 recipes in this book, this Strawberry Pretzel Salad Pie just may be one of my favorites! Give it a try and you'll understand! **8–10 SLICES**

INGREDIENTS

FOR CRUST

Cooking spray

1¼ cups crushed pretzels

8 tablespoons (1 stick) unsalted butter, melted

3 tablespoons brown sugar

FOR FILLING & TOPPING

Two 8-ounce packages cream cheese, at room temperature

½ cup sugar

1 tablespoon pure vanilla extract

One 8-ounce tub frozen whipped topping, such as Cool Whip, thawed

One 21-ounce can strawberry pie filling (see Note)

NOTE: You can substitute the canned pie filling with fresh strawberries, if preferred. Just put 2 cups of sliced fresh strawberries in a medium bowl and add 1 cup of sugar. Mix well and allow to rest until syrupy.

1. Prepare the crust: Lightly spray a 9-inch-diameter pie plate with cooking spray. Combine the crushed pretzels, melted butter, and brown sugar in a medium bowl until moistened and combined. Press into the prepared pie plate until compact. Set aside.

2. Prepare the filling and topping: Cream together the cream cheese, sugar, and vanilla in a large bowl, using an electric mixer, until smooth and creamy, about 2 minutes. Fold in the whipped topping until the whole mixture is combined and fluffy.

3. Spread the cream cheese mixture on the crust, smoothing out the top. Refrigerate for at least 4 to 6 hours or until set. Just before serving, spoon the strawberry pie filling evenly over the top of the pie before cutting into slices.

Brownie Bottom Banana Cream Pie

I'm sure you've had banana cream pie before, and if you're like me, it's one of your favorites. But if you are indeed like me, you also enjoy mixing things up. Living on the edge, pushing the limits, breaking the rules, and other metaphors like that. That means when you eat banana cream pie, you also think, man, this could really be improved with a brownie on the bottom, because naturally, your thought process is always about outdoing the food in front of you. Welcome to my world! 8–10 SLICES

INGREDIENTS

FOR BROWNIE BOTTOM

1 box brownie mix (for an 8-inch square pan), plus ingredients listed on back of package

One 9-inch deep-dish frozen piecrust (see Note)

FOR FILLING

1½ cups banana slices

1 box instant banana pudding mix

2 cups milk

One 8-ounce tub frozen whipped topping, such as Cool Whip, thawed

Additional whipped cream and miniature chocolate chips for garnish (optional but recommended)

NOTE: I recommend using a deep-dish crust because a regular crust cannot accommodate all of the filling. If you only have a regular-size crust on hand, fill the crust with the filling just about to the top rim of the crust and eat the remaining filling!

1. Prepare the brownie bottom: Preheat your oven to 350°F. Prepare the brownie mix according to the package directions and pour the brownie batter into the bottom of the piecrust. Bake for 25 to 30 minutes, until a toothpick inserted near the center of the brownie comes out clean. Remove from the oven and allow to cool completely.

2. Prepare the filling: Whisk together the banana pudding mix and milk until thickened, about 2 minutes. Fold in the whipped topping until fluffy and combined.

3. Take the banana slices and layer on top of the brownie. Spread the banana pudding filling over the banana slices and smooth out the top. Refrigerate for at least 6 hours to set.

4. Just before serving, top with whipped cream and miniature chocolate chips.

5

Cereal Sweets and Treats

My love for cereal knows no bounds. Whether I'm eating it with milk in a bowl, or, well, straight from the box—I love the stuff! This chapter is filled with sweets and treats made with my favorite cereals. Enjoy!

Cinnamon Cereal Cookies

My love of cinnamon comes from my mom, who basically taught me that the only way to eat toast is with copious amounts of butter and about ½ cup of cinnamon sugar per slice. I put cinnamon on just about everything, which makes it not surprising when I say that Cinnamon Toast Crunch cereal is one of my favorites! There's something so intoxicating about those crispy squares that has me craving it at least once a week. If you like cinnamon (hi, we're now best friends), you'll flip for these cookies!

34 COOKIES

INGREDIENTS

FOR COOKIES

16 tablepoons (2 sticks) unsalted butter, at room temperature

¾ cup brown sugar

¼ cup granulated sugar

1 large egg

1 large egg yolk

2 teaspoons pure vanilla extract

1 teaspoon baking soda

¼ teaspoon salt

2 cups all-purpose flour

1 tablespoon milk powder

1 box instant vanilla pudding mix

1 cup Cinnamon Toast Crunch or similar cereal, finely crushed

FOR GLAZE

1 cup confectioners' sugar

3 to 4 tablespoons milk

1 teaspoon pure vanilla extract

1. Preheat your oven to 350°F. Line two baking sheets with parchment paper or silicone liners; set aside.

2. Cream together the butter, brown sugar, and granulated sugar in a large bowl, using an electric mixer, until creamy, about 1 minute. Beat in the egg, egg yolk, and vanilla until combined. Beat in the baking soda, salt, flour, milk powder, and vanilla pudding mix until a soft dough forms. Beat in the crushed cereal.

3. Drop rounded tablespoon-size balls of dough 2 inches apart on the prepared baking sheets. Bake for 8 to 10 minutes, rotating the pans halfway through the baking time to ensure they're evenly baked. Remove from the oven and allow to cool on the baking sheets.

4. Once the cookies have cooled, prepare your glaze: Whisk together the confectioners' sugar, milk, and vanilla in a small bowl until smooth. Drizzle over each cookie and allow the glaze to set, about 10 minutes, before serving.

Marshmallow Charms Ice Cream

I used to work this terribly boring office job, answering phones for ten hours a day. When I wasn't daydreaming about food, shopping, or literally anything else, I was shoveling handfuls of Lucky Charms into my mouth; I considered them my special treat every shift and would keep a box in my desk. My favorite part, of course, was the dehydrated marshmallows. Those little things are the best part! When I was creating recipes for this chapter, I knew I had to combine this cereal with ice cream, which is a way better mix-in than regular old milk! 1 QUART (4 CUPS)

INGREDIENTS

3 cups heavy cream

2 cups Lucky Charms or similar cereal

¼ cup sugar

One 14-ounce can sweetened condensed milk

2 cups cereal marshmallows (see Note)

NOTE: You can find cereal marshmallows (the exact Lucky Charms marshmallows, minus the cereal!) online or in specialty food stores. They are used in other recipes, such as Marshmallow Charms Bundt Cake (page 136) and Marshmallow Charms Pudding Pie (page 147). In a pinch, enlist a kid to help you pick the marshmallows from a standard box of cereal!

1. Soak the Lucky Charms cereal in the cream for 1 hour. Strain the cereal from the cream and pour the cream into a large bowl. Add the sugar.

2. Whip together the cereal-flavored cream and sugar in a large bowl, using an electric mixer on high speed, until stiff peaks form, about 5 minutes. Fold in the sweetened condensed milk to combine, then fold in the cereal marshmallows.

3. Pour into a freezer-safe container and cover. Freeze for 8 hours, or until firm.

Crunchy Cereal Milk Shake

Since I'm a food blogger, I'm always on the hunt for unique eats and treats during my travels. The last time I went to New York City (a.k.a. the best place in the world!), I tried a local hot spot that is notorious for over-the-top milk shakes. I'm talking about slices of cake sitting atop skyscraper-size glasses of milk shakes. So naturally, I had to re-create an out-of-control milk shake for this book, because if I didn't, I would be depriving you of greatness. Check out the Red Velvet Cupcake Shake (page 170), too!

2–4 GLASSES, DEPENDING ON THE SIZE

INGREDIENTS

2 cups vanilla ice cream

1 cup milk

2½ cups Cap'n Crunch or similar cereal

1 tablespoon instant milk powder

1 cup canned or homemade vanilla frosting

1. Place the ice cream, milk, 1½ cups of the cereal, and the milk powder in a blender. Blend on high speed for 1 minute or until the mixture is smooth.

2. Spread the vanilla frosting on the outside rim of two to four glasses. Dredge the frosting-rimmed glasses in the remaining cup of cereal.

3. Divide the milk shake equally among the glasses. Serve immediately.

Marshmallow Charms Bundt Cake

I am obsessed with my Bundt pan. It's been through the ringer with me, it's put up with my whimsical cake ideas, and although it's let me down before by not releasing my cake, we always make up in the end. I know this sounds weird, writing a mini monologue about my Bundt pan, but I tell ya—it's one of my favorite pans to use! It helps make this cake into the star that it is, with its whimsy and magical qualities that only charm cereal has.

12 SERVINGS

INGREDIENTS

Cooking spray

1 cup cereal marshmallows (see Note)

One 11.5-ounce box Lucky Charms or similar cereal

2 cups Rice Krispies or similar cereal

Two 10-ounce bags miniature marshmallows

8 tablespoons (1 stick) unsalted butter

NOTE: You can find cereal marshmallows (the exact Lucky Charms marshmallows, minus the cereal!) online or in specialty food stores.

1. Spray a 10-cup Bundt pan with cooking spray. Sprinkle the cereal marshmallows evenly along the bottom of the pan. Toss the cereals together in a large bowl and set aside.

2. Melt the miniature marshmallows and butter together in a large saucepan over medium-low heat, stirring constantly. Once melted, pour the hot marshmallow mixture into the bowl of mixed cereals. Toss together until the cereal is fully coated.

3. Spoon the cereal mixture into the prepared pan and press down gently to compact, using greased hands. Let set for 2 to 3 hours.

4. Just before serving, use a butter knife to run around the edges of the pan to gently release the cake.

Fruity Cereal Cupcakes

Growing up, we always had sugary cereal on hand. So, it's no surprise that my love for the stuff has basically been in my DNA since my birth. My parents were never health nuts that ate bran cereal with skim milk—my dad alone could put down a box of Froot Loops in one sitting as if it was his job. I really wanted to make sure I included a Froot Loops recipe in this book since it was a cornerstone of my childhood, and I'm so glad I did! There is no shortage of cereal goodness in these! **18–20 CUPCAKES**

INGREDIENTS

FOR CUPCAKES

1 box white cake mix

1¼ cups milk

3 large eggs

½ cup vegetable oil

1 box instant vanilla pudding mix

2 cups Froot Loops or similar cereal, plus more for garnish

FOR FROSTING

16 tablespoons (2 sticks) unsalted butter, at room temperature

1 tablespoon dry milk powder

1 teaspoon pure vanilla extract

¼ teaspoon almond extract

3 cups confectioners' sugar

¼ cup heavy cream

2 to 3 drops blue or green food coloring (optional)

1. Preheat your oven to 350°F. Line a muffin pan with 18 paper liners. Combine the milk and 1 cup of the cereal in a liquid measuring cup; let sit for 15 minutes, then strain the milk, discarding the cereal.

2. Beat together the cake mix, cereal milk, eggs, oil, and vanilla pudding mix in a large bowl, using an electric mixer, for 2 minutes, or until smooth. Crush the remaining cup of cereal in a large resealable plastic bag until finely ground, then mix the ground cereal crumbs into the cake batter.

3. Portion the cake batter evenly among the muffin cups, filling about three-quarters full. Bake for 16 to 18 minutes, until a toothpick inserted near the center comes out clean or with moist crumbs. Remove from the oven and allow to cool completely.

4. Prepare the frosting: In the bowl of a stand mixer, cream together the butter, dry milk powder, and vanilla and almond extracts until creamy, about 1 minute. Add the confectioners' sugar, 1 cup at a time, beating well after each addition. Stream in the cream if the frosting is too thick. Finally, add the food coloring, if using, and beat to combine.

5. Pipe or frost the cupcakes and garnish with any remaining cereal.

Frosted Cereal Fried Ice-Cream Sundaes

I cannot believe that I had been deprived of fried ice cream for so long! I had it as an adult and it's been a favorite ever since. Little did I know how easy it is to make at home, if not a little bit messy. But now that I know I can whip it up at home, you bet your bottom dollar I'm going to be making it constantly. What I love about this recipe is that it's totally versatile. Here, I used caramel and vanilla swirled ice cream, but you could use chocolate, peanut butter cup, black cherry—really any flavor! The Frosted Flakes and toffee bits that crust each ice-cream scoop give it a wonderful crunch without the deep fry. **14 SERVINGS**

INGREDIENTS

One 1.5-quart container caramel vanilla ice cream

3 cups Frosted Flakes or similar cereal

1½ teaspoons ground cinnamon

½ cup toffee bits

Chocolate syrup, caramel sauce, and cherries (optional)

1. Line a baking sheet with parchment paper. Scoop out ½-cup portions of ice cream into ball shapes and place them on the baking sheet. Freeze for 2 hours, or until solid and firm.

2. Crush the cereal in a large resealable plastic bag until coarse. Mix the cereal crumbs with the ground cinnamon and toffee bits in a shallow bowl.

3. Dredge the ice-cream scoops into the cereal mixture one at a time, coating all sides evenly. Place back on the baking sheet and freeze again for another 2 hours or until firm.

4. Serve with chocolate syrup, caramel sauce, and cherries, if desired.

Peanut Butter Cereal Popcorn

My brother and sister love peanut butter cups. As kids, I would always trade them my peanut butter cups for their Almond Joys and without fail, they'd accept the trade. It wasn't until I was older that I tried peanut butter cups again and realized what I'd been missing out on. I was also older when I first tried Reese's Puffs cereal, which made me go through a period of making up for lost time by eating it daily for like a month straight. This popcorn provides all that delicious peanut butter cup flavor, whether you're new to loving the candy or it's been an old favorite. **10 CUPS**

INGREDIENTS

8 cups plain or lightly buttered popped popcorn

2 cups Reese's Puffs or similar cereal

One 16-ounce package vanilla candy coating (also known as vanilla almond bark)

2 tablespoons creamy peanut butter

2 cups miniature peanut butter cups

1. Line a baking sheet with parchment paper and set aside. Toss together the popped popcorn and cereal in a large, heatproof bowl until combined. Set aside.

2. Microwave the vanilla candy coating in a medium bowl according to the package directions or until smooth. Whisk in the peanut butter to blend. Pour the candy mixture over the popcorn mixture and toss until the popcorn mixture is thoroughly coated. Toss in the peanut butter cups.

3. Spread the popcorn mixture evenly on the prepared baking sheet and allow the coating to set, about 30 minutes, before breaking into pieces and serving.

Fruity Cereal No-Bake Cheesecake

Fruity Pebbles are my favorite cereal of all time. There's something about those fruity little shards of cereal goodness. When I was in high school, some days I'd come home after school and eat several bowls of cereal before I tackled my homework. Best. Decision. Ever. Maybe that's the secret to getting straight As? Let's just go with that. In my first book, *Out of the Box Desserts*, I made a similar cheesecake to this one, only with toasted marshmallow flavors and a cocoa cereal crust. This version is nice and fruity, and guaranteed to please! **12 SERVINGS**

INGREDIENTS

FOR CRUST

6 cups Fruity Pebbles or similar cereal

8 tablespoons (1 stick) unsalted butter, plus more for glass

One 10-ounce bag miniature marshmallows

Cooking spray

FOR FILLING & TOPPING

One 8-ounce package cream cheese, at room temperature

½ cup sugar

1 teaspoon pure vanilla extract

One 7-ounce jar marshmallow fluff

One 8-ounce tub frozen whipped topping, such as Cool Whip, thawed

1 cup cherry pie filling (about ½ [21-ounce] can)

1. Prepare the crust: Pour the cereal into a large, heatproof bowl and set aside. Melt the butter and miniature marshmallows together in a saucepan over medium heat until smooth. Pour the hot marshmallow mixture over the cereal and toss until fully coated.

2. Spray a 9-inch springform pan with cooking spray. Press the cereal mixture into the prepared pan. I think it's easiest to use the buttered bottom of a glass to help press and compact the cereal crust in the pan and up the sides. Let set for 20 minutes.

3. Prepare the filling: Cream together the cream cheese, sugar, and vanilla in a large bowl, using an electric mixer, for 1 minute or until creamy. Beat in the marshmallow fluff until combined, then fold in the whipped topping until combined completely.

4. Pour the cheesecake filling into the cereal crust and smooth out the top. Refrigerate until set, about 2 hours. Just before serving, top with the cherry pie filling.

Marshmallow Charms Pudding Pie

Pudding pies are one of the easiest recipes you can make. Simply fold together the pudding, milk, and whipped topping and you're ready to go! This pie's extra-special because it's flavored just like Lucky Charms! The last time I went to New York City, I stopped at a place called Milk Bar. Milk Bar is known for its cereal milk soft-serve, which gave me the idea to infuse cereal milk into the pudding mixture. This totally ramps up the cereal flavor and makes it extra-creamy, rich, and delicious. **8 SERVINGS**

INGREDIENTS

1½ cups milk

1½ cups Lucky Charms or similar cereal

1 box instant vanilla pudding mix

One 8-ounce tub frozen whipped topping, such as Cool Whip, thawed

One 9-inch graham cracker crust

1 cup cereal marshmallows (see Note)

Additional whipped cream for topping pie (optional)

NOTE: You can find cereal marshmallows (the exact Lucky Charms marshmallows, minus the cereal!) online or in specialty food stores.

1. Mix together the milk and cereal in a medium bowl and refrigerate uncovered for 1 hour to absorb the flavors. After an hour, strain the cereal from the milk. You should now have about 1 cup of milk.

2. Whisk together the pudding mix and cereal milk in a large bowl until thickened, about 2 minutes. Fold in the whipped topping to combine.

3. Spread the mixture on the prepared graham cracker crust and smooth out the top. Refrigerate for at least 6 hours or overnight.

4. Just before serving, spread the cereal marshmallows around the edges or on the top of the pie. Garnish with additional whipped cream, if using.

Peanut Butter Cup Krispy Rice Tart

My mom never made crispy rice treats while I was growing up. Her reason (and it wasn't to torture me)? She hates getting messy. Ribs, wings, and these treats are all off the table because of the stickiness that surrounds them. For that reason, I was deeply deprived of my favorite treat. The only time I ever had a chance to sink my teeth in that gooey, crispy bar is when my mom bought the premade ones that, let's face it, aren't the same. I knew I had to create a crispy rice treat–inspired goodie for this book, and this tart—which combines chewy, crisp cereal, marshmallows, and peanut butter cups—certainly delivers! 12 SERVINGS

INGREDIENTS

Cooking spray

6 cups Rice Krispies or similar cereal

4 tablespoons (½ stick) unsalted butter, plus more for glass

One 10-ounce bag miniature marshmallows

1½ cups semisweet chocolate chips

¼ cup creamy peanut butter

¼ cup heavy cream

One 11-ounce bag Reese's Miniature Peanut Butter Cups or similar candies, chopped

1. Spray a 9- or 10-inch round tart pan with cooking spray. Place the cereal in a large, heatproof bowl and set aside.

2. Over medium heat, melt the butter and miniature marshmallows together in a saucepan until smooth. Pour the hot marshmallow mixture over the cereal and toss until fully coated. Press the cereal mixture into the tart pan. I think it's easiest to use the buttered bottom of a glass to help press and compact the cereal mixture into the tart pan. Let set for 20 minutes.

3. Microwave the chocolate chips, peanut butter, and cream together in a medium microwave-safe bowl on HIGH for 30 seconds. Stir, and then continue to microwave in 15-second increments until smooth and melted.

4. Pour the chocolate mixture over the surface of the tart. Immediately top with the chopped peanut butter cups. Let set for 20 minutes, and then cut into slices.

Avalanche Cookies

As a teenager, I'd beg my parents to take me to the mall on the weekends with my friends. Sometimes, if I was lucky, they'd drop me off in downtown Sacramento to wander and explore. Without fail, my friends and I would head to Old Town, where the streets are cobblestoned and the shops are novelty. We'd hang out in the gag gift shop, and then make our way to the chocolate shop on the corner. I'd always order an Avalanche Bar: loaded with crispy rice cereal, marshmallows, a peanut buttery white chocolate mixture, and chocolate chips, it was so worth the allowance money I spent on it. These are a cookie version of those crispy, gooey bars . . . and dare I say, they're even better than the real thing! **20–24 COOKIES**

INGREDIENTS

2 cups Rice Krispies or similar cereal

2 cups miniature marshmallows

One 16-ounce package vanilla candy coating (also known as vanilla almond bark)

½ cup creamy peanut butter

1 cup miniature chocolate chips

1. Line a baking sheet with parchment paper and set aside. Toss together the cereal and miniature marshmallows in a large, heatproof bowl.

2. Microwave the candy coating in a large bowl according to the package directions or until smooth. Whisk in the peanut butter to combine.

3. Pour the candy coating mixture over the cereal and toss until completely coated. Working quickly, drop rounded spoonfuls of the mixture onto the prepared baking sheet. While the cookies are still wet, sprinkle with miniature chocolate chips. Let the cookies set, about 15 minutes, before serving.

S'mores Graham Cereal Bars

Even though I loathe camping (I actually prefer getting flu shots over camping . . . by a lot), I love s'mores. They just remind me of snuggling up by a cozy fire . . . indoors, of course. Although I rarely eat an actual s'mores, I love making other desserts that taste like s'mores without the fire-setting business. These cookie bars taste just like a good old-fashioned s'more but in an easy, portable bar. And bonus: you can eat them indoors. **15 BARS**

INGREDIENTS

Cooking spray

6 cups Golden Grahams or similar cereal

4 tablespoons (½ stick) unsalted butter

One 10-ounce bag miniature marshmallows

2 cups semisweet chocolate chips

¼ cup heavy cream

1. Lightly spray a 9-×-13-inch rectangular pan with cooking spray. Place the cereal in a large, heatproof bowl and set aside.

2. Melt the butter and miniature marshmallows together in a saucepan over medium heat until smooth. Pour the hot marshmallow mixture over the cereal and toss to coat completely. Press the cereal mixture into the prepared pan. Let set for about 1 hour at room temperature or 30 minutes in the fridge.

3. Microwave the chocolate chips and cream together in a small microwave-safe bowl on HIGH for 30 seconds. Stir, then microwave again in 15-second increments until melted and smooth. Pour the chocolate mixture evenly over the bars, spreading to cover to the edges. Let the chocolate set for about 20 minutes in the fridge before cutting into bars.

Fruity Cereal Ice-Cream Sandwiches

Obviously you've heard of crispy rice treats made from different types of cereal, right? But did you know you can make ice-cream sandwiches out of the treats, too? It's a total game-changer, and these ice-cream sandwiches will make history, I'm sure of it. The best part is you can switch up the ice cream and cereal flavors to create awesome new combinations. While these are stuffed with vanilla bean ice cream, they'd be incredible with strawberry ice cream, too! **4 SANDWICHES**

INGREDIENTS

Cooking spray

6 cups Fruity Pebbles or similar cereal

4 tablespoons (½ stick) unsalted butter

One 10-ounce bag miniature marshmallows

2 cups (1 pint) vanilla bean ice cream, slightly softened

NOTE: This recipe can easily be doubled! Other flavor options are chocolate cereal paired with mint chocolate chip ice cream, peanut butter–flavored cereal paired with peanut butter ice cream, or fruit-flavored cereal paired with bubble-gum-flavored ice cream.

1. Lightly spray a 9-×-13-inch rectangular pan with cooking spray. Place the cereal in a large, heatproof bowl and set aside.

2. Melt the butter and miniature marshmallows together in a saucepan over medium heat until smooth. Pour the hot marshmallow mixture over the cereal and toss to coat completely. Press the cereal mixture into the prepared pan. Let set for about 1 hour at room temperature or 30 minutes in the fridge.

3. Using a 3-inch round cookie cutter, cut circles from the cereal mixture. You should have eight circles. Place on the prepared baking sheet.

4. Flip four of the cereal circles over and top each with ½ cup of slightly softened ice cream. Take another cereal circle and gently press it on top of the ice-cream half. Immediately freeze for 4 hours or until firm.

Caramel Rocky Road Cereal Bars

Rocky road is a flavor combination I often forget about. Maybe it's because, as a kid, I couldn't stand the stuff—the idea of anything but sprinkles or cookie dough in my ice cream was off the table. But as an adult, I realized how amazing rocky road actually is. Chocolate, nuts, and marshmallows make for one killer holy trinity in dessert cooking. These bars combine with caramel candies for an extra layer of gooey goodness. Try to say no to this one! **15 BARS**

INGREDIENTS

Cooking spray

6 cups Cocoa Krispies or similar cereal

4 tablespoons (½ stick) unsalted butter

One 10-ounce bag miniature marshmallows

1 cup chopped walnuts

1 cup chopped Rolo or similar caramel candies

1. Lightly spray a 9-×-13-inch rectangular pan with cooking spray. Place the cereal, walnuts, and ½ cup of the chopped candy in a large, heatproof bowl and set aside.

2. Melt the butter and miniature marshmallows together in a saucepan over medium heat until smooth. Pour the hot marshmallow mixture over the cereal and toss to coat completely. Press the cereal mixture into the prepared pan and sprinkle the top with the remaining ½ cup of chopped candy. Allow to cool at room temperature for about 1 hour before cutting into squares.

Fluffernutter Muddy Buddies

Whenever it was lunchtime in my house, my dad would offer to make us sandwiches. He knew we'd always say no, but he'd always ask if we wanted a fluffernutter for lunch. When I was older, I actually tried marshmallow and peanut butter together and it was kinda life-changing. Sweet, salty, and totally addictive. I was determined to make as many fluffernutter-inspired desserts as humanly possible. These muddy buddies (also known as puppy chow, for reasons I don't know) combine the sweetness of marshmallows and the salty crunch of peanuts and peanut butter for one delightful snack mix. Eating it for lunch is recommended! **8 CUPS**

INGREDIENTS

One 16-ounce package vanilla candy coating (also known as vanilla almond bark)

¼ cup creamy peanut butter

8 cups Rice Chex or similar cereal

2½ cups confectioners' sugar

2 cups unsalted peanuts

2 cups miniature marshmallows

1. Microwave the candy coating in a large bowl according to the package directions, stirring until smooth and melted. Whisk in the creamy peanut butter. Add the cereal to the bowl, tossing to coat the cereal completely with the peanut butter mixture.

2. Place the confectioners' sugar in a gallon-size resealable plastic bag. Pour the coated cereal into bag, seal it, and shake the bag vigorously to coat all the cereal with the confectioners' sugar.

3. Add the peanuts and marshmallows to the plastic bag and shake to combine.

Cinnamon Cereal Cupcakes

I used to work at a cupcake shop many moons ago. One of my favorite cupcakes we sold was the snickerdoodle cupcake. Cinnamon-flavored cupcakes topped with a buttery frosting . . . is there anything better? And now on my blog, my Churro Cupcakes are now one of my most popular recipes. So the universe was basically begging me to create my own cereal–inspired version for this book, and here it is! A cinnamon cupcake topped with a cereal buttercream frosting. Trust me, there is nothing better than this version! **18 CUPCAKES**

INGREDIENTS
FOR CUPCAKES

1 box white cake mix

1/3 cup vegetable or canola oil

1¼ cups milk

3 large eggs

1 box instant vanilla pudding mix

2 teaspoons ground cinnamon

FOR FROSTING & GARNISH

12 tablespoons (1½ sticks) unsalted butter, at room temperature

¾ cup Cinnamon Toast Crunch or similar cereal crumbs

1 teaspoon pure vanilla extract

3 cups confectioners' sugar

¼ cup heavy cream or milk

18 Cinnamon Toast Crunch or similar cereal pieces

1. Prepare the cupcakes: Preheat your oven to 350°F. Line a muffin tin with 18 paper liners; set aside.

2. Beat together the cake mix, oil, milk, eggs, vanilla pudding mix, and cinnamon in a large bowl, using an electric mixer, until smooth and blended, about 2 minutes.

3. Portion the batter equally among the prepared muffin cups, filling about three-quarters full. Bake for 16 to 18 minutes, until a toothpick inserted near the center comes out clean or with moist crumbs. Remove from the oven and allow to cool completely.

4. Prepare the frosting: Cream together the butter, cereal crumbs, and vanilla in a large bowl, using an electric mixer, until creamy, about 1 minute. Gradually add the confectioners' sugar, about 1 cup at a time, until light and fluffy. If the frosting is too thick, stream in the cream until soft and spreadable.

5. Pipe or frost the cupcakes with the frosting and top each with a Cinnamon Toast Crunch piece.

6

Frozen and No-Bake Desserts

Everyone loves a good no-bake dessert, right? When the temperature rises, it's so miserable to turn on the oven to bake something. This chapter is chock-full of no-bake recipes that will cool you down, perk you up, and of course, leave your oven off!

Peach Cobbler Ice Cream

I'll be the first to tell you I'm not the biggest peach fan in the world . . . but in this ice cream? I'm all about peaches! They just evoke such a feeling of summertime: warm temperatures, blue skies, juicy peaches. A.k.a., heaven! You can usually find me during summer months inside under the AC vent, sipping a peach iced tea and eating a big bowl of this stuff. Something fabulous happens when you combine peach pie filling with ice cream; just try it and see for yourself! 1 QUART (4 CUPS)

INGREDIENTS

2 cups heavy cream

½ cup brown sugar

1 teaspoon pure vanilla extract

One 14-ounce can sweetened condensed milk

8 chewy oatmeal cookies, roughly chopped

1 teaspoon ground cinnamon

One 21-ounce can peach pie filling, chopped

NOTE: Not a peach fan? This ice cream would be lovely with apple pie filling, or even cherry pie filling!

1. Whip together the cream, brown sugar, and vanilla in a large bowl, using an electric mixer on high speed, until stiff peaks form, 5 to 7 minutes.

2. Gently fold the sweetened condensed milk into the whipped cream mixture until fully incorporated. Fold in the chopped oatmeal cookies, cinnamon, and the chopped peach pie filling until blended.

3. Pour the ice-cream mixture into a resealable container with a lid and freeze for at least 8 hours, preferably overnight, before serving.

Cake Batter Dessert Dip

Have you ever been invited to a party, asked to bring something, and forgotten until the last minute? Yeah, me too. And because I'm such a baking goddess, people expect me to bring the latest and greatest dessert all the time . . . which is a lot of pressure, if you wondered! So, when I need to whip something up in a flash that's sure to disappear, I make this Cake Batter Dessert Dip. Serve it alongside graham crackers, fresh fruit, sugar cookies—whatever!—and you'll be the goddess at your next party! **2½ CUPS**

INGREDIENTS

½ cup white chocolate chips

¼ cup heavy cream

One 8-ounce package cream cheese, at room temperature

⅔ cup confetti cake mix (just the dry powder)

1 teaspoon pure vanilla extract

½ teaspoon almond extract

One 7-ounce jar marshmallow fluff

½ cup rainbow sprinkles, plus more for topping (optional)

Graham crackers, fresh fruit, sugar cookies, and/or pretzels for dipping

1. Microwave the white chocolate chips and cream together in a microwave-safe bowl on HIGH for 20 seconds. Stir, then microwave again for another 10 seconds. Stir until smooth and melted. Allow to cool for 15 minutes.

2. Beat together the cream cheese, confetti cake mix, and vanilla and almond extracts in a large bowl, using an electric mixer, until combined and smooth. Beat in the melted white chocolate mixture until combined. Finally, beat in the marshmallow fluff. The mixture will be thick and fluffy. Fold in the rainbow sprinkles.

3. Pour into a small dish and top with additional sprinkles, if desired. Cover and refrigerate for at least 1 hour before serving.

Gooey Butter Cake Ice Cream

Okay, so I fibbed—but it was only a small fib, I promise! This recipe does require some baking, but I pinkie-promise it's more than worth it! Gooey butter cake is a St. Louis staple, but since I've never been to Missouri, I figured I'd bring it to me! This ice cream is filled with real chunks of gooey butter cake swirled throughout, which makes for one seriously scrumptious ice cream! 1 QUART (4 CUPS)

INGREDIENTS

FOR CAKE

Cooking spray

1 box yellow cake mix

4 large eggs

16 tablespoons (2 sticks) unsalted butter, melted

One 8-ounce package cream cheese, at room temperature

One 16-ounce box confectioners' sugar

1 teaspoon pure vanilla extract

FOR ICE CREAM

2 cups heavy cream

One 14-ounce can sweetened condensed milk

1 teaspoon pure vanilla extract

1. Prepare the cake: Preheat your oven to 350°F. Line a 9-×-13-inch rectangular baking pan with foil, extending the sides of the foil over the edges of the pan. Spray the foil liberally with cooking spray.

2. Stir the cake mix, one of the eggs, and ½ cup of the melted butter in a large bowl, until moistened and combined. Press the cake mixture evenly into the bottom of the prepared pan; set aside.

3. Beat the cream cheese in a large bowl, using an electric mixer on medium speed, until smooth. Beat in the remaining three eggs, one at a time, beating well after each addition, followed by the entire pound of confectioners' sugar and the vanilla. With the mixer on low speed, stream in the remaining ½ cup of melted butter to combine.

4. Pour the filling evenly over the cake "crust" and bake for 38 to 42 minutes, until the cake is just about done. Allow to cool completely, then refrigerate for at least 2 hours. Once chilled, cut the bars in half. Save one half for another use (such as eating it plain) and cut the remaining half into 1-inch cubes.

5. Prepare the ice cream: Whip the cream in a large bowl, using an electric mixer on high speed, until stiff peaks form, 5 to 7 minutes. Fold in the condensed milk and vanilla gently, until fully incorporated. Toss in the cake cubes and gently fold to combine.

6. Spread the ice-cream mixture into a resealable container with a lid. Freeze for at least 8 hours, preferably overnight.

Red Velvet Cupcake Shake

Shakes are no longer just a simple milk shake in a glass. That's so passé. Nowadays, milk shakes are topped high with insane toppings, such as a pound of candy, gigantic peanut butter cups, or slices of cheesecake. And this shake is no exception to the new trend. Topped with a huge mountain of fluffy whipped cream and garnished with an entire red velvet cupcake (not to mention the entire red velvet cake slice in the shake!), it's perfect for red velvet cake lovers who want their cake . . . and ice cream, too!

2–4 GLASSES

INGREDIENTS

One 3-inch square or slice of prepared and iced red velvet cake or cupcake

2 cups vanilla or sweet cream ice cream

1½ cups milk

Whipped cream, chocolate sprinkles, chocolate syrup, and additional red velvet cupcakes for garnish (optional but recommended)

NOTE: To make the cupcakes sit upright on the glass, peel off the cupcake liner and gently make a slit in the middle of the bottom side of a cupcake, careful not to cut all the way through. Slip the cupcake onto the rim of the glass.

1. Blend together the slice or square of red velvet cake, the ice cream, and the milk in a large blender, about 1 minute or until mostly smooth.

2. Pour into two to four glasses, depending on how large your glasses are. In the photo, mine are large hurricane-style glasses that yielded me two milk shakes. Top with chocolate syrup, whipped cream, chocolate sprinkles, and an additional red velvet cupcake as a garnish before serving, as desired.

Peanut Butter and Jelly Tiramisu

This may be one of my favorite recipes in the book because it's so unique and unexpected! Everyone and their mama have had tiramisu before, but have you ever eaten tiramisu with a grade-school twist? I promise, not only kiddos will like this tiramisu, but the adults will be instantly transported back to grade school (without the awkwardness, homework, or being picked on by that bully named Billy) with this fun twist! Not to mention, it has Twinkies in it, so you know it's gonna be good! **9–12 SLICES**

INGREDIENTS

10 Twinkies or similar snack cakes, split lengthwise

1 cup seedless raspberry jam, warmed

One 12-ounce tub whipped cream cheese

½ cup creamy peanut butter

½ cup sugar

1 teaspoon pure vanilla extract

One 8-ounce tub frozen whipped topping, such as Cool Whip, thawed

Fresh raspberries for garnish

1. Line an 8- or 9-inch square baking pan with foil, extending the sides of the foil over the edges of the pan. Lay half of the split Twinkies (a total of 10 Twinkie halves) on the bottom of the baking dish in an even layer. Spread half of the warm jam evenly over the Twinkies.

2. Beat together the whipped cream cheese, peanut butter, sugar, and vanilla in a large bowl until blended and smooth, about 2 minutes. Fold in the whipped topping until fluffy and combined. Spread half of the peanut butter mixture evenly over the jam layer in the pan. Top with the remaining Twinkie halves lined up evenly, followed by the remainder of the warm jam and the remaining peanut butter mixture. Garnish with the fresh raspberries.

3. Cover and refrigerate for at least 4 hours to set before cutting into squares to serve.

Candy Bar Squares

Snickers are probably the most popular American candy bar, no? I remember in high school, everyone was noshing on Snickers bars during lunch and breaks because our school café sold them for really cheap. Ah, the food for the mind: chocolate and nougat. But because of Snickers' success, I knew I had to make something inspired by the stuff, so these squares were born. Chewy, gooey, crunchy, and melt-in-your-mouth buttery, they're a can't-miss recipe if you love Snickers as much as America does! **15–18 SQUARES**

INGREDIENTS

Cooking spray

6 cups Rice Krispies or similar cereal

10 cups miniature marshmallows

4 tablespoons (½ stick) unsalted butter, plus more for glass

1½ cups chopped dry-roasted peanuts

One 11-ounce bag caramel bits

¾ cup heavy cream

1½ cups milk chocolate chips

1. Lightly spray a 9-×-13-inch rectangular baking pan with cooking spray; set aside.

2. Place the cereal and 2 cups of miniature marshmallows in a large bowl and set aside. Meanwhile, melt the remaining 8 cups of miniature marshmallows and the butter together in a large saucepan over medium-low heat until smooth and melted, 3 to 5 minutes. You can also microwave the miniature marshmallows and butter in a large microwave-safe bowl on HIGH until melted, 40 to 60 seconds. Pour the melted marshmallow mixture evenly over the cereal mixture and toss to combine.

3. Press the cereal mixture into the bottom of the prepared pan and use the bottom of a buttered drinking glass to compact the cereal mixture into the pan.

4. Melt the caramel bits and ¼ cup of the cream together in a small saucepan over medium-high heat until smooth and melted, about 5 minutes. Pour the caramel mixture evenly over the cereal bars and spread to the edges. Immediately sprinkle with the chopped peanuts. Refrigerate for 1 hour.

5. Microwave the remaining ½ cup of cream and the milk chocolate chips in a small microwave-safe bowl on HIGH for 30 seconds. Stir, then melt again for another 10 to 15 seconds. Stir until melted and smooth. Pour the melted chocolate mixture evenly over the caramel layer and smooth to the edges. Refrigerate for another 30 minutes, or until set, before cutting into squares.

Banana Split Lush Dessert

Lush desserts are one of my very favorite things to make on my blog and for my family. For one, they're super ridiculously easy, and for two, the flavor combinations are infinite, which makes it fun to concoct new flavors! This Banana Split Lush Dessert combines rich banana pudding with classic banana split ice-cream flavors into one simple, no-bake treat. One bite and you'll be hooked, too! 9–12 SLICES

INGREDIENTS

Cooking spray

One 14.3-ounce package Golden Oreo or similar cookies, coarsely crushed

8 tablespoons (1 stick) unsalted butter, melted, plus more for glass

One 21-ounce can strawberry pie filling

1 box instant banana pudding mix

1 cup milk

One 8-ounce tub frozen whipped topping, such as Cool Whip, thawed

Whipped cream and miniature chocolate chips for garnish

1. Lightly spray an 8- or 9-inch square baking pan with cooking spray. Combine the coarsely crushed cookies and the melted butter in a bowl until moistened. Press the cookie mixture into the bottom of the prepared pan, gently compacting it as tightly as possible with the bottom of a buttered glass or by using your hands. Spread the strawberry pie filling evenly over the surface of the cookie crust; set aside.

2. Whisk together the banana pudding mix and milk in a large bowl until thickened, about 2 minutes. Fold in the whipped topping until fluffy and combined.

3. Spread the banana pudding mixture evenly over the strawberry pie filling layer. Top with additional whipped cream and miniature chocolate chips and refrigerate, uncovered, for at least 6 to 8 hours or overnight, until set, before cutting into squares.

Sinful Brookie Icebox Cake

Even though my parents didn't cook while I was growing up, I wish they'd known about icebox cakes because they're one of the easiest things on the planet to make, *and* you can enlist children to help make it! Traditional icebox cakes use regular Oreos throughout the whole thing, but since this is a riff on Sinful Brookies (Oreos + chocolate chip cookies + brownies), I knew I had to up the ante by a million. This isn't diet-friendly, but it sure is taste bud–friendly! 20–24 SLICES

INGREDIENTS

One 13-ounce package chocolate chip cookies, such as Chips Ahoy

4½ cups milk

1 box instant vanilla pudding mix

1 box instant chocolate pudding mix

One 14.3-ounce package Oreo or similar cookies

One 8-ounce tub frozen whipped topping, such as Cool Whip, thawed

2 cups Brownie Brittle or similar, coarsely crushed

Chocolate syrup for garnish

1. Dip the chocolate chip cookies one by one into a dish of ½ cup of the milk and lay them in rows in a 9-×-13-inch rectangular baking pan. You may use only 20 to 22 of the chocolate chip cookies; save the rest for another use! Reserve the dish of milk for step 3.

2. Whisk together the vanilla pudding mix and 2 cups of the milk in a medium bowl until smooth. Pour evenly over the chocolate chip cookie layer. Wipe out the bowl and set aside.

3. Dip the Oreo cookies one by one into the milk dish and lay them in rows on top of the vanilla pudding layer. You will likely use all of the Oreos.

4. Whisk together the chocolate pudding mix and remaining 2 cups of milk in a medium bowl until smooth. Pour evenly over the Oreo layer. Spread the whipped topping on top of the chocolate pudding layer and top with the crushed Brownie Brittle and chocolate syrup.

5. Refrigerate for at least 4 hours or until set before cutting into squares.

Crème Brûlée Ice Cream

Truth: I have never made crème brûlée at home before. I don't have a kitchen torch, which is a pretty important component to making a successful crème brûlée. One, because I'm afraid of fire and a fire-blowing torch sounds like the last thing I need; and two, because I can barely wield a curling iron with finesse. There's no way I can operate a culinary flame-thrower without being second-degree burned. But I learned I can just as easily re-create those amazing crème brûlée flavors at home without firepower. This ice cream is proof of that! 1 QUART (4 CUPS)

INGREDIENTS

2 cups heavy cream

½ cup confectioners' sugar

2 vanilla beans, seeds scraped and reserved

One 14-ounce can sweetened condensed milk

1½ cups toffee bits

1. Whip together the heavy cream, confectioners' sugar, and vanilla bean seeds in a large bowl, using an electric mixer on high speed, until stiff peaks form, 5 to 7 minutes. Gently fold in the sweetened condensed milk until incorporated. Fold in ½ cup of the toffee bits.

2. Pour half of the ice-cream mixture into a resealable container with a lid; sprinkle with ½ cup of the toffee bits. Top with the remainder of the ice-cream mixture and the remaining ½ cup of toffee bits. Freeze for at least 8 hours, preferably overnight, before serving.

Chocolate Chip Cookie Dough Pudding

I'm going to let you in on a little secret: scratch-made pudding is not as hard as I believed it to be. I thought it would require the wisdom and experience of a great-grandmother who has been whipping up homemade pudding for decades. But you don't have to be wise, experienced, or a great-grandmother (or even female, for that matter!) to whip up a creamy, smooth pudding that tastes just like cookie dough. This pudding has a wonderful brown sugar base that's folded with chocolate chips and served with cookies on the side to drive home that delicious cookie dough point.

4 CUPS

INGREDIENTS

½ cup brown sugar

3 tablespoons cornstarch

¼ teaspoon salt

2 cups whole milk, cold

1 teaspoon pure vanilla extract

2 tablespoons unsalted butter

2 cups miniature chocolate chips

Chocolate chip cookies for garnish

1. Whisk together the brown sugar, cornstarch, and salt in a medium saucepan until combined. Whisk in the cold milk. Place over medium-low heat and cook until thickened, 5 to 7 minutes, and until the mixture coats the back of a metal spoon. Do not allow the mixture to boil.

2. Remove from the heat and whisk in the vanilla and butter until smooth. Spoon the pudding into a bowl and press plastic wrap directly into the pudding's surface and up the sides of the bowl. Chill in the fridge for at least 2 hours or until set.

3. Just before serving, fold in the chocolate chips. Spoon into glasses and serve with chocolate chip cookies.

Brownie Batter Mousse

I remember the first time I tried chocolate mousse. I was a kid and was grocery shopping with my mom when I noticed a box of mousse mix in the store. I had had pudding before, but never pudding's foreign, fancier cousin, and was immediately intrigued. One bite was all it took to get me hooked on this fluffy, airy, heavenly treat. This version uses brownie mix to create an ultralight, super brownie-packed dessert, all entirely no-bake! **4 CUPS**

INGREDIENTS

1½ cups miniature marshmallows

8 ounces bittersweet chocolate, chopped

½ cup milk

2 cups heavy cream

1 cup brownie mix (just the dry powder)

Additional whipped cream, fresh raspberries, or Brownie Brittle for garnish

1. Melt the miniature marshmallows, chopped chocolate, and milk together in a medium saucepan over medium-low heat, stirring constantly, until smooth and melted. Remove from the heat and allow to cool completely.

2. Whip the heavy cream in a large bowl, using an electric mixer on high speed, until stiff peaks form. Beat in the dry brownie mix until combined.

3. Fold the chocolate marshmallow mixture into the whipped cream mixture until combined and smooth. Spoon into glasses and refrigerate for at least 3 hours before serving. Just before serving, garnish with additional whipped cream, fresh raspberries, or Brownie Brittle if desired.

Vanilla Snack Cake Truffles

One of the treats my family regularly stock-piled growing up were Twinkies. Golden, light-as-air snack cakes filled with that irresistible cream filling. I remember sneaking into my grandma's bottom cupboard and snatching a Twinkie when she was busy watching her soap operas in the next room, then army-crawling back to the den where I'd savor every bite of that spongy cake. Now, I prefer to enjoy my Twinkies in truffle form. Like cake pops but *so much easier*, they're a little bite that reminds me of my childhood. **12–16 TRUFFLES**

INGREDIENTS

10 Twinkies or similar vanilla snack cakes

One 10-ounce package white melting chocolates, such as Ghirardelli

Yellow food coloring

1. Place all 10 Twinkies in a large bowl. Using your hands, smash and knead the Twinkies together to form a cohesive mixture. The mixture should be moistened and slightly sticky.

2. Form tablespoon-size balls of the Twinkie mixture and round them out with your hands. Place on a foil-lined baking sheet. Freeze the truffles for at least 1 hour or until firm.

3. Melt the white melting chocolate according to the package directions, or until melted and smooth. Reserve one-quarter of the chocolate mixture in a small bowl.

4. Dip the truffles into the white chocolate, using a fork to gently submerge the truffle. Lift the fork and allow the excess to drip off. Return the coated truffle to the baking sheet and repeat with the remaining truffles.

5. Tint the reserved white chocolate with one or two drops of yellow food coloring until a pale yellow shade has been achieved. Pour the now yellow chocolate into a plastic sandwich bag, seal out the air, and snip off the tip of a lower corner of the bag. Drizzle the yellow chocolate over the truffles. Let set before serving.

Ice-Cream Sandwich Cake

Summers at my house were spent lounging by the pool lazily and eating my weight in ice-cream sandwiches. We always got the classic kind because there's something very nostalgic about a good old-fashioned ice-cream sandwich, am I right? This Ice-Cream Sandwich Cake combines those classic sandwiches with Oreos to create a delicious and simple treat for those sweltering summer days. Lounging poolside is optional, but recommended. 8–10 SLICES

INGREDIENTS

9 to 11 store-bought ice-cream sandwiches

3 cups whipped cream or frozen whipped topping, such as Cool Whip (thawed)

10 Oreo or similar cookies, coarsely crushed

1. Line an 8- or 9-inch rectangular loaf pan with parchment paper, extending the sides of the parchment over the edges of the pan. Place three to four ice-cream sandwiches into the bottom of the pan, cutting the sandwiches, if necessary, to fit in the gaps. Top with 1 cup of whipped cream and a sprinkling of Oreo cookie crumbs.

2. Layer twice more as before with the ice-cream sandwiches, whipped cream, and cookie crumbs.

3. Freeze for 8 hours or overnight, until firm and solid. To remove, gently lift the parchment paper overhang and slice.

Miscellaneous Sweets

Not quite cupcakes, and not quite cookies, the sweets that make up the rest of the book are fantastic treats, including Apple Fritter Bread Pudding, Cookie Truffle Brownie Bombs, Animal Cookie Fudge, and more!

Brownie Truffle "Fries"

When I first saw something similar to these on the menu at one of my favorite burger restaurants, I had to give them a try. Sweet, salty, and ultrarich, they're fudge brownies coated in chocolate and sprinkled with sea salt for a little crunch. The restaurant served the fries with raspberry jam for a dipping "sauce" and that was pure brilliance. No matter how you eat them, if you're a superfudgy brownie fan, these are a must-make! **10–12 BROWNIE "FRIES"**

INGREDIENTS

Cooking spray

12 tablespoons (1½ sticks) unsalted butter, cubed

2 ounces bittersweet chocolate, chopped

1½ cups sugar

1 teaspoon pure vanilla extract

2 large eggs

½ cup unsweetened cocoa powder

1 cup all-purpose flour

½ teaspoon salt

One 16-ounce package chocolate candy coating (also known as almond bark)

Flaked sea salt

1. Preheat your oven to 350°F. Line an 8- or 9-inch square baking pan with foil, extending the sides of the foil over the edges of the pan. Spray the foil liberally with cooking spray.

2. Microwave the butter and bittersweet chocolate together in a medium microwave-safe bowl on high for 25 seconds. Stir, then continue to melt for 10 seconds. Stir until smooth and melted. Allow to cool for about 15 minutes.

3. Whisk in the sugar, vanilla, and eggs until combined. Whisk in the cocoa powder, flour, and salt until the brownie batter comes together. Pour the batter into the prepared pan and smooth out the top.

4. Bake the brownies for 22 to 25 minutes, until a toothpick inserted near the center comes out clean or with moist crumbs. Remove from the oven and allow to cool completely. Once cooled, cut the brownies in half crosswise, then cut them into strips lengthwise. You should get anywhere from 10 to 12 strips, depending on how large you cut them. Freeze the brownie strips on a foil-lined rimmed baking sheet until solid, about 30 minutes.

5. Melt the chocolate candy coating according to the package directions or until smooth. Dip each frozen brownie fry into the chocolate, coating it completely and allowing any excess chocolate to drip off. Return the fry to the baking sheet and immediately sprinkle with flaked sea salt. Repeat with remaining brownie fries.

Caramel Apple Fruit Pizza

There's a little area near my home in Sacramento called Apple Hill. It's up in the foothills and surrounded by fragrant apple orchards that have been there since the 1960s. We try to go every year because it's such a fun departure from suburbia, and because of everything apple flavored. My favorite treats to get (besides the piping hot apple donuts) are caramel apples, dipped in their homemade caramel sauce. To this day, caramel apples remain one of my favorite sweets, and they are the star of this easy and impressive pizza!

12–14 SLICES

INGREDIENTS

Cooking spray

One 24-count package refrigerated sugar cookie dough, at room temperature

One 8-ounce package cream cheese, at room temperature

¼ cup brown sugar

1 teaspoon pure vanilla extract

4 ounces (½ [8-ounce] tub) frozen whipped topping, such as Cool Whip, thawed

2 to 3 medium apples, cored and chopped into bite-size pieces (see Note)

1 cup chopped pecans

1½ cups caramel sauce

NOTE: I used a mixture of Granny Smith and Gala apples because those are my favorite types. Use all Granny Smith or any apple combinations or varieties you prefer.

1. Preheat your oven to 350°F. Lightly spray a 9-inch round springform pan with cooking spray. Place a parchment round in the bottom of the pan and spray again. Press the cookie dough into the prepared pan in an even layer.

2. Bake for 20 to 25 minutes, until the top is golden brown and appears set in the middle. Remove from the oven and allow to cool completely, then release from the pan and place the cookie layer on a cake stand or platter.

3. Beat together the cream cheese, brown sugar, and vanilla in a large bowl, using an electric mixer, until smooth, about 2 minutes. Fold in the whipped topping until fluffy and combined. Spread the mixture evenly over the surface of the cookie. Top with the chopped apples and chopped pecans, and drizzle liberally with the caramel sauce. Serve immediately.

Oatmeal Scotchie Peach Cobbler

One of my favorite cookies growing up was called an Oatmeal Scotchie. A buttery, hearty oatmeal cookie studded with butterscotch chips . . . the perfect balance of sweet, a little salty, and chewy, just like a cookie should be. This peach cobbler has a cookie-rific update: Oatmeal Scotchie cookies as the cobbler topping! And if you've never tried a cookie-topped fruit cobbler, this is your lucky day! 12–15 SERVINGS

INGREDIENTS

Cooking spray

One 18-ounce box Oatmeal Scotchie cookie mix, such as Krusteaz

8 tablespoons (1 stick) unsalted butter, at room temperature

1 large egg

2 teaspoons ground cinnamon

Two 21-ounce cans peach pie filling (see Note)

NOTE: You can replace canned pie filling with 4 cups peeled and sliced fresh or thawed frozen peaches tossed with ¾ cup brown sugar and 2 teaspoons ground cinnamon.

1. Preheat your oven to 375°F. Liberally spray a 9-×-13-inch rectangular baking dish with cooking spray.

2. Mix together the cookie mix, butter, egg, and cinnamon in a medium bowl until combined. Pour the peach pie filling into the prepared pan in an even layer. Dollop the cookie dough evenly over the surface of the peach pie filling.

3. Bake for 25 to 35 minutes, or until the cookie top has set and the filling is bubbly.

Apple Fritter Bread Pudding

Sometimes, if we were lucky, my parents would take us to get donuts on weekend mornings at the little donut shop up the road. I always went with a sugar donut, because the one thing a donut is missing is extra sugar. My dad, however, always went for the apple fritter—one the size of his palm, craterlike in appearance, and stuffed with apples. I didn't appreciate how good an apple fritter truly was until I was older, and now they're a staple whenever I go to any new donut shop. This bread pudding is made with chopped-up apple fritters, because it is, after all, the one thing bread pudding needs. **12–15 SERVINGS**

INGREDIENTS

Cooking spray

2 tablespoons unsalted butter, melted

6 to 8 medium-size apple fritters, chopped into bite-size pieces (see Note)

One 21-ounce can apple pie filling, chopped (see Note)

4 large eggs, beaten

2 cups milk

¾ cup brown sugar

1 tablespoon pure vanilla extract

2 teaspoons ground cinnamon

½ teaspoon ground nutmeg

1½ cups confectioners' sugar

½ cup apple cider

NOTE: You can use any glazed donut for this recipe! Just omit the pie filling.

NOTE: You can substitute the canned pie filling with fresh apples, if preferred. Just peel and dice 4 cups of Granny Smith apples and sauté them with 3 tablespoons brown sugar, 2 teaspoons ground cinnamon, ¼ teaspoon ground nutmeg, and ¼ teaspoon ground ginger, in 2 tablespoons unsalted butter for 5 minutes.

1. Preheat your oven to 350°F. Liberally spray a 9-×-13-inch rectangular baking pan with cooking spray. Spread the pie filling into the prepared pan. Place the apple fritter cubes evenly on top and drizzle with the melted butter. Set aside.

2. Whisk together the eggs, milk, brown sugar, 2 teaspoons of the vanilla, and the cinnamon and nutmeg in a large bowl until combined and smooth. Pour the mixture evenly over the apple fritter cubes and gently toss the cubes around in the mixture so they're thoroughly moistened.

3. Bake, covered, for 15 minutes, then carefully remove the foil and continue to bake for 40 minutes, or until the bread pudding is set. Remove from the oven and let cool for 15 minutes.

4. Whisk together the confectioners' sugar, remaining teaspoon of vanilla, and the apple cider in a small bowl until smooth. Pour evenly over the bread pudding before serving.

Milk and Cookies Scones

I'm a big breakfast food fan. Whenever I have the chance to go out to eat breakfast, I am on it like gravy on biscuits. It's kind of hard to choose what I like the most, but dessertlike breakfasts are up there. (Are you surprised?!) Whether it is donuts (an obvious choice), French toast, waffles, or scones, I really love it all. These scones could be enjoyed at breakfast time, but they have a definite dessert twist that makes them uniquely over the top . . . and perfect any time of day! **8 SCONES**

INGREDIENTS

3 cups all-purpose flour

6 tablespoons granulated sugar

3 tablespoons brown sugar

1 teaspoon salt

4½ teaspoons baking powder

8 tablespoons (1 stick) unsalted butter, cold

1²/₃ cups heavy cream

2 teaspoons pure vanilla extract

2 cups chopped chocolate chip cookies

²/₃ cup miniature chocolate chips

1. Preheat your oven to 400°F. Line a cookie sheet with parchment paper or a silicone liner; set aside.

2. Toss together the flour, granulated sugar, brown sugar, salt, and baking powder in a large bowl until blended. Grate the butter into the flour mixture, using a cheese grater. Gently toss the flour mixture and butter together until moistened and crumbly. Make a well in the center of the flour mixture and pour in 1⅓ cups of the cream and the vanilla. Slowly incorporate the flour mixture into the liquid until the dough is just coming together and slightly shaggy. Do not overmix, as this will lead to tough scones! Just before it comes together, fold in the cookies until just barely combined.

3. Sprinkle a little flour onto a flat surface and knead the dough gently, folding it in and over itself once or twice. Pat the dough into a flattened disk about 8 inches in diameter. Cut into eight equal pieces. Separate the pieces and place on the prepared baking sheet. Brush with the remaining ⅓ cup of cream.

4. Bake for 15 to 18 minutes, until golden brown and set. Remove from the oven and allow to cool slightly before serving or serve at room temperature.

Brownie Pudding

This isn't your mama's instant pudding, honey. This is a whole new level of pudding awesomeness. If you want to get technical, it's kind of like a cross between pudding and cobbler. Strange, I know—but man, does it work beautifully together. This cake is best served warmed up and piled with ice cream and chocolate sauce . . . because how else would you serve it?

9 SERVINGS

INGREDIENTS

Cooking spray

1 box fudge brownie mix

1 teaspoon baking powder

½ cup milk

1/3 cup vegetable or canola oil

1 large egg

1 teaspoon pure vanilla extract

1 box instant chocolate pudding mix

1 cup hot water

Ice cream, chocolate syrup, and additional toppings for garnish

1. Preheat your oven to 350°F. Liberally spray a 9-inch square baking pan with cooking spray and set aside.

2. Mix together the brownie mix, baking powder, milk, oil, egg, and vanilla extract in a medium bowl until combined. Pour the batter into the prepared pan. Sprinkle the chocolate pudding mix evenly over the top of the batter, then pour the hot water on top of the pudding mix.

3. Carefully place the dish in the oven and bake for 30 to 40 minutes or until the brownie portion looks set. Parts of the dish may look underdone, but that's the "pudding" part of the dish.

4. Remove from the oven and allow the dish to cool for about 15 minutes before serving. Garnish with ice cream, chocolate sauce, and any other additional toppings.

Pumpkin Pie Cannoli

I am embarrassed to say, but for a long time, I wasn't a pumpkin pie fan. Whenever it was dished up at Thanksgiving, I would request a piece . . . with about 1 cup of whipped cream on top. I'd then take my whipped cream–smothered piece of pie and head to the living room, where I'd proceed to scrape all the whipped cream off and into my mouth, then return the piece of uneaten pie to the table. (I was a pleasant child; why do you ask?). But now I enjoy the flavor of pumpkin pie, and I enjoy it even more in cannoli form! Because, let's face it—not enough things are cannoli-fied. **12 CANNOLI**

INGREDIENTS

One 8-ounce tub whipped cream cheese, at room temperature

½ cup sugar

¾ cup pure pumpkin purée

2 teaspoons pumpkin pie spice

1 teaspoon pure vanilla extract

One 8-ounce tub frozen whipped topping, such as Cool Whip, thawed

12 cannoli shells (see Note)

NOTE: You can find unfilled cannoli shells at some specialty food stores or online. Can't find cannoli shells? The pumpkin pie filling would make an excellent dip! Serve with fresh fruit, waffle cookies, graham crackers, or brownie bites.

1. Beat together the whipped cream cheese and sugar in a large bowl, using an electric mixer, until creamy, about 1 minute. Beat in the pumpkin purée, pumpkin pie spice, and vanilla until combined. Fold in the whipped topping until the mixture is light and fluffy.

2. Pipe the pumpkin filling mixture into each cannoli shell. I like to spoon the pumpkin mixture into a gallon-size resealable plastic bag, snip off the corner, and use the bag to pipe the mixture in.

3. Serve the cannoli immediately.

Pecan Pie Baklava Bites

If you're a frequent party-hoster or partygoer, these would be an awesome treat to serve to guests. Syrupy, pecan-filled, crispy morsels of pure decadence, they are. And way easier to whip up than traditional baklava! No one has to know it's only a few simple ingredients . . . **15 BAKLAVA BITES**

INGREDIENTS

One 15-count package frozen phyllo cups

2 tablespoons unsalted butter, melted

¼ cup dark corn syrup

½ teaspoon pure vanilla extract

¼ teaspoon ground cinnamon

2 tablespoons brown sugar

1 cup chopped pecans

1. Preheat your oven to 350°F. Line a rimmed baking sheet with foil or parchment paper and place the phyllo cups onto the baking sheet, spaced about 1 inch apart. Set aside.

2. Whisk together the melted butter, dark corn syrup, vanilla, cinnamon, and brown sugar in a medium bowl until combined. Fold in the pecans and toss to coat.

3. Drop rounded tablespoonfuls of the pecan mixture into each phyllo cup, filling to the brim. Bake the baklava bites for 10 minutes or until bubbly and slightly golden brown.

4. Serve at room temperature or warmed. This recipe can be easily doubled!

Donut Strawberry Shortcakes

People often think that food bloggers are wizards in the kitchen . . . and in many ways, we are. But sometimes it's hard coming up with recipes off the top of your head. It's like a real-life game of the TV show *Chopped*, only we don't need to use wasabi or scorpion lollipops to make cupcakes (thankfully). While I was coming up with the recipes for this book, I knew I wanted a strawberry shortcake recipe but with a fanciful update. And then it dawned on me: Donuts were just the right amount of fanciful I need! And the rest is history. (Also, no scorpions were used in this recipe. Promise.)

6 SHORTCAKES

INGREDIENTS

6 glazed yeast or cake donuts, split in half crosswise

1 pint fresh strawberries, cored and sliced

½ cup granulated sugar

1½ cups heavy cream

⅔ cup confectioners' sugar

1. Place a bottom donut half onto a plate and repeat with remaining donuts and plates. Set the tops aside.

2. Toss together the sliced strawberries and granulated sugar in a bowl until fully coated and let sit for 10 minutes. Meanwhile, whip together the heavy cream and confectioners' sugar in a large bowl, using an electric mixer on medium-high speed, until stiff peaks form, 5 to 7 minutes.

3. Pipe or spoon a little whipped cream onto each doughnut half; top with a spoonful of strawberries. Add a little more whipped cream and top it off with the remaining donut half. Repeat with the remaining donuts. Serve immediately.

Hot Chocolate Fudge

Hot chocolate is one of those beverages I often forget how much I love. I know that sounds weird—as if you can't forget someone you love that easily—but you can, because I've seen it happen in movies and why would Hollywood lie to me? Anyway, once I take a sip of that creamy, chocolaty goodness, I'm instantly transformed into a happier, cozier human being. This Hot Chocolate Fudge evokes those same feelings of coziness . . . and will make for an unforgettable new love affair with fudge. **36 PIECES**

INGREDIENTS

Cooking spray

2 cups milk chocolate chips

One 14-ounce can sweetened condensed milk

1 teaspoon pure vanilla extract

1 tablespoon instant hot cocoa powder

1 cup miniature marshmallow bits (see Note)

NOTE: The miniature marshmallow bits are a product by Kraft Jet-Puffed. They're superteeny dehydrated marshmallows found either in the baking aisle near the marshmallows or in the hot cocoa aisle near the cocoa powder.

1. Line an 8- or 9-inch square baking pan with foil, extending the sides of the foil over the edges of the pan. Mist the foil lightly with cooking spray. Set aside.

2. Melt the chocolate chips and sweetened condensed milk together in a medium saucepan over medium-low heat, stirring constantly, until melted and smooth. Stir in the vanilla and hot cocoa powder until combined.

3. Pour the mixture into the prepared pan and smooth out the top. Top liberally with the miniature marshmallow bits.

4. Refrigerate the fudge for at least 4 hours before cutting into pieces.

Turtle Candy Brownie Bombs

Can we all agree that the "turtle" flavor profile is extremely underrated? And by "turtle," I'm definitely not referring to those shelled dudes who move slowly. I'm referring to the caramel-chocolate-pecan business that's frequently seen in ice cream, brownies, and candies. I love turtle-flavored treats because the combination of gooey caramel, rich chocolate, and crunchy pecans is unbeatable. And thankfully for you, it's the star of these brownie bombs: fudgy baked brownies filled with caramel candies, coated in chocolate and topped with pecans. Oh yes, indeed. 40 BROWNIE BOMBS

INGREDIENTS

One 9-×-13-inch pan fudge brownies, baked and cooled (see Note)

40 Rolo or similar caramel candies, unwrapped

One 16-ounce package chocolate candy coating (also known as almond bark)

40 pecan halves

NOTE: I highly recommend using Pillsbury's Chocolate Fudge Brownie Mix for your brownie bombs. I've tested lots of different mixes, and this one is by far the best. You are welcome to use your own favorite homemade fudge brownie recipe, too!

1. Trim the tough, crispy edges from the brownies in the pan, then cut the brownies (minus the edges) into 40 equal squares.

2. Take a piece of brownie and gently flatten it in the palm of your hand. Place a Rolo candy in the middle of the brownie and use your hands and fingers to gently wrap the brownie around the candy, rolling it in your palms to cover the candy completely with the brownie. Place on a parchment-lined baking sheet and repeat with remaining brownies.

3. Freeze the brownie bombs for at least 1 hour, or until firm. Once they are frozen solid, melt the candy coating according to the package directions, until smooth and melted.

4. Dip each brownie bomb into the melted chocolate candy coating, using a fork. Allow any excess chocolate to drip off, then return the coated brownie bomb to the baking sheet. Immediately top with a pecan half. Repeat with remaining brownie bombs.

5. Allow the chocolate candy coating to set before serving. Bring the brownie bombs close to room temperature before serving, as the caramel candy inside needs to thaw from being frozen.

Animal Cookie Fudge

One of my weaknesses (besides dress shopping, bad reality TV featuring housewives, and Coke Zero with light ice, among many things) happens to be Circus Animal Cookies. They're a staple from my childhood, when my brother and I would divide them up by color and munch on them while watching *Scooby Doo*. I could have sworn the white ones tasted better, which is weird seeing that I love the color pink so much. But what I didn't know then was that the cookies—both pink and white—would taste a million times better sitting in a plate of vanilla fudge. With age comes infinite wisdom, I suppose! **36 PIECES**

INGREDIENTS

Cooking spray

2 cups white chocolate chips

One 14-ounce can sweetened condensed milk

1 teaspoon pure vanilla extract

2 cups chopped Circus Animal or similar cookies

¼ cup rainbow nonpareil sprinkles

Pink food coloring

1. Line an 8- or 9-inch square baking pan with foil, extending the sides of the foil over the edges of the pan. Mist the foil lightly with cooking spray. Set aside.

2. Melt the white chocolate chips and sweetened condensed milk together in a medium saucepan over medium-low heat, stirring constantly, until melted and smooth. Stir in the vanilla until combined. Pour ½ cup of the fudge mixture into a separate bowl and tint the bowl of fudge pink.

3. Mix 1 cup of the chopped cookies into the white fudge and pour the mixture into the prepared pan, smoothing out the surface. Top with dollops of the pink fudge scattered at random, then use a butter knife to swirl the two colors together. Top with the remaining cup of cookies and the sprinkles.

4. Refrigerate the fudge for at least 4 hours before cutting into pieces.

Cookie Truffle Brownie Bombs

I'm sure you've had an Oreo ball before: ground-up Oreos mixed with cream cheese and covered in chocolate. But because it's me, I kind of had to one-up the classic Oreo ball and make a Cookie Truffle Brownie Bomb happen, because I aim to please. These brownie bombs are filled with a delightful, creamy Oreo truffle, covered by a fudge brownie and coated in chocolate. The result is pure decadence . . . and dare I say, better than the original! 22–24 BROWNIE BOMBS

INGREDIENTS

25 Oreo or similar cookies

4 ounces cream cheese, at room temperature

One 9-x-13-inch pan fudge brownies, baked and cooled

1 teaspoon instant espresso powder

One 16-ounce package chocolate candy coating (also known as almond bark)

NOTE: Don't limit yourself to regular-flavored Oreos! These would be excellent with mint Oreos, peanut butter Oreos, or one of their seasonal varieties.

1. Pulverize 20 of the cookies in a food processor until finely ground. Pulse in the cream cheese and espresso powder until the mixture comes together and is moistened and cohesive. Roll the mixture into tablespoon-size balls and place on a parchment- or silicone-lined baking sheet. Freeze for 1 hour or until firm.

2. Trim the tough, crispy edges from the brownies in the pan, then cut the brownies (minus the edges) into 24 equal squares.

3. Take a piece of brownie and gently flatten it in the palm of your hand. Place an Oreo truffle in the middle of the brownie and use your hands to wrap the brownie around the truffle, rolling it in your palms to cover the truffle completely. Place on a parchment-lined baking sheet and repeat with the remaining brownies.

4. Freeze the brownie bombs for at least 1 hour or until firm. Once they are frozen solid, melt the candy coating according to the package directions until smooth and melted. Crush the remaining Oreos with the back of a spoon until they resemble coarse crumbs; set aside.

5. Dip each brownie bomb into the melted chocolate candy coating, using a fork. Allow any excess chocolate to drip off, then return the coated brownie bomb to the baking sheet. Immediately top with some of the coarsely crushed Oreo crumbs. Allow the chocolate to set before serving.

HANDY CONVERSIONS

1 cup	8 fl oz	16 Tbsp	48 tsp	237 ml
¾ cup	6 fl oz	12 Tbsp	36 tsp	177 ml
⅔ cup	5 fl oz	11 Tbsp	32 tsp	158 ml
½ cup	4 fl oz	8 Tbsp	24 tsp	118 ml
⅓ cup	3 fl oz	5 Tbsp	16 tsp	79 ml
¼ cup	2 oz	4 Tbsp	12 tsp	59 ml
⅛ cup	1 oz	2 Tbsp	6 tsp	30 ml

TO DOUBLE A RECIPE

1 cup	2 cups
½ cup	1 cup
⅓ cup	⅔ cup
¼ cup	½ cup
1 Tbsp	2 Tbsp
1 tsp	2 tsp
¾ tsp	1½ tsp
¼ tsp	½ tsp

TO CUT A RECIPE IN HALF

1 cup	½ cup
½ cup	¼ cup
⅓ cup	8 tsp
¼ cup	2 Tbsp
1 Tbsp	1½ tsp
1 tsp	½ tsp
¾ tsp	⅜ tsp
½ tsp	¼ tsp
¼ tsp	⅛ tsp

Acknowledgments

I'd like to thank my mom and dad for encouraging me to believe in my dreams, as corny and clichéd as that sounds. You raised me to believe I could be anything I wanted to be—even when that dream changed weekly—and encouraged me to continue writing, which I found to be my real passion. Your support is mind-blowing and my love for you two is immeasurable. Thank you.

Thank you to my brother, Alex, and my sister, Chloe, for supporting me along the way as well. Alex, thanks for letting me utilize your design aesthetic in deciding which bowl or specific fork looked best in a photo and thank you for taste-testing fudge, and decadent desserts first thing after waking up because I was too anxious to wait. And thanks to you, Chloe, for getting me Coke Zeros when I was furiously working away and you could tell by my old pajamas and crazy hair that I maybe needed some caffeinated assistance. And also for taste-testing a million things, a lot of which was chocolate, which I know you don't like. So, thank you!

Thank you to my friends who have checked in on me during the writing process, making me laugh and feel included, despite the fact that I was working as a recluse for the last five months. Your support means a lot to me. The blogging world is very cut-throat, but I'm glad I can count on a few wonderful ladies to bring me up when I'm down.

Thank you to Sara Hawkins, my amazing superwoman lawyer who yet again made my life when she said I was writing yet *another* cookbook. Having you in my corner makes life so much easier!

Thank you to Ann Treistman, Devorah Backman, Aurora Bell, and Becca Kaplan for making my experience of writing two books with The Countryman Press such a dream come true. You ladies are whip-smart, book savvy, and your knowledge, support, and help has been invaluable to me.

Thank you to my three pups, Mannie, Jack, and Winston, for your unconditional love always and forever. I love you more than you know!

And most important, a big, mushy THANK YOU to all the readers of this book and of my blog, *The Domestic Rebel*. Your support is so encouraging and motivates me to think outside the box to create one-of-a-kind desserts and hilarious stories for you, on the page and on the screen. Thank you for subscribing to my blog; for all your likes, comments, and shares; for pinning my recipes; for your uplifting comments; and for buying my books! YOU are the reason I continue to do this! YOU ROCK!

XOXO, Hayley

Index